A BIRDWATCHIN

MALLC

GRAHAM HEARL and JON KING

ARLEQUIN PUBLICATIONS

ISBN 09522019 76

First published 1995

Arlequin Press, 26 Broomfield Road, Chelmsford, Essex CM1 1SW
Telephone: 01245 267771
© Graham Hearl and Jon King

A catalogue record for this book is available.

CONTENTS

Acknowledgements

The inspiration for this guide was provided by Pat Bishop and her late husband Eddie Watkinson, and we, along with all birdwatchers visiting the island, owe them both a huge debt of gratitude for all they have done to encourage birdwatching on Mallorca. We thank all those Mallorquins, far too numerous to mention by name, who allow us access to their property, enabling us to birdwatch so enjoyably on their island. Many resident bird-watchers on Mallorca, both Mallorquin and English, have provided us with ideas and information over the years, for which we are very grateful. Many thanks to Beatriz Arroyo who commented on drafts of the manuscript, and provided two of the vignettes.

Introduction

Birdwatching abroad has come a long way since the boom in tourism in the early 1970's, with cheap air transport and birder-oriented package holidays enabling many exotic destinations to come within comparatively easy reach. Mallorca was one of the first destinations to become popular with birdwatchers from northern Europe who relished the opportunity to get to grips with the impressive migrations of the Mediterranean and with the localised breeding birds of the area. To be able to do this in rather better climates than they were used to at home was of course a major advantage. Mallorca is extremely well-serviced with international flights, politically stable, and has an infrastructure geared to tourism. Above all, with no point on the island more than 100 km from any other, it is very compact, with a large range of habitats from high mountains to lowland marshes and coastal scrub all within reach on the same day, if desired. The obvious birdwatching potential of such an area was first realised by Eddie Watkinson, whose publication of "A Guide to Birdwatching in Mallorca" in the 1970's did much to fuel the huge upsurge in ornithological interest on the island. Eddie's book has now been out of print for many years, yet Mallorca remains as popular as ever with foreign birdwatchers, and many hundreds still visit the island every year.

On an island that has seen as many changes as Mallorca has over the last twenty or so years, access information for visitors needs constant updating. That the Albufera Marsh would one day become a Natural Park was a distant dream in the 1970's, but now it is firmly established and managed, with an impressive network of hides and well-marked paths. Albercutx Valley is now inaccessible, the once-excellent Ternelles Valley is very difficult of access, and the Bocquer Valley seems perpetually under threat of going the same way. Tucan Marsh has all but gone. The list of building projects on or near the Albufereta seems never-ending, yet it is also widely mooted as Mallorca's next Natural Park. With so many changes having occurred in the recent past, a comprehensive revision of the Watkinson guide has long been necessary, and this book is intended to fill that gap. Furthermore, and partly thanks to the interest generated by Eddie's book, our knowledge of Mallorcan birds has developed equally rapidly over the last decade or so. This greatly improved knowledge is reflected in the forthcoming publication in the Poyser series of "Birds of the Balearic Islands" (King and Hearl, in prep). A checklist to the birds of Mallorca, with simplified status comments, is consequently provided towards the back of this book.

Birds in Mallorca, and when to stay

Mallorca is an ideal holiday destination for the keen birdwatcher, whether an expert wanting to get to grips with such specialities as Eleonora's Falcon, Marmora's Warbler and Audouin's Gull, or for a first trip abroad, with the island offering an excellent introduction to southern European birds, with a spectacular passage of migrants in spring, repeated to a lesser extent in the autumn. The ideal time to visit is therefore from mid-April to mid-May, but any time of the year can be rewarding as Mallorca also holds good numbers of birds in winter, retreating from the extremes of weather on the European mainland. Despite the heat in high summer, there are always odd late spring or early autumn migrants to be seen, together with the resident and summering species.

As any good travel agent should be able to supply information on to how to get to Mallorca, we will make no attempt here to discuss this topic. There are innumerable package deals available, as well as flight-only deals should you prefer to make your own accommodation arrangements. It is also possible to get to Mallorca by car from the U.K., but as this makes the cost for a one or two week holiday prohibitive, it is much cheaper to hire.

The resident species for which Mallorca is best-known are Black Vulture, Audouin's Gull, Marmora's Warbler, Thekla Lark, and Blue Rock Thrush, and it is possible to see all these species at any time of the year in their appropriate habitats, although in mid-winter you may have to travel to the south of the island to guarantee seeing Audouin's Gull. Other species present throughout the year and of particular interest to visiting birders include Mediterranean Shearwater, Little and Cattle Egrets, Night Heron, Booted Eagle, Crag Martin, Moustached Warbler, Sardinian Warbler, Serin, Crossbill (of the endemic sub-species *balearica*), Black-winged Stilt, Kentish Plover and the recently reintroduced Purple Gallinule and Red-crested Pochard.

Winter is the time to see concentrations of wildfowl in wetland areas, with Shoveler, Teal, Wigeon, Pintail and Tufted Duck in abundance; plus a spectacular Starling flock at S'Albufera (up to one million birds), wintering thrushes, Black Redstarts, Black-necked Grebe, Cattle Egrets, up to three wintering Great White Egrets, and a few Alpine Accen-tors to be found mainly on the mountain tops.

Spring is the most popular time for birders, when migration is in full swing. In early spring it is still possible to see many of the wintering species, as well as early migrants such as Montagu's Harrier, Black-eared Wheatear, hirundines, chats, some warblers, Garganey, waders such as Wood Sandpiper, and the locally breeding migrants such as Purple Heron, Woodchat Shrike and Subalpine Warbler. Cory's and Mediterranean Shear-water are to be seen in numbers at this time of the year from all the headlands, especially the Cabo de Salinas.

It is necessary to wait until the second half of April to see the following (in addition to those mentioned above): marsh terns, more waders including Marsh Sandpiper, Golden Oriole, flycatchers, and summer visitors like Short-toed Lark and Tawny Pipit. To be really sure of seeing Eleonora's Falcon and Bee-eater it is best to wait until the very end of April. Squacco Heron, Honey Buzzard and Red-footed Falcon are also more likely into May. It is at this time that the island is filled with the song of Nightingales.

In early summer nesting is well under way; Rock Thrush and Spectacled Warbler can be seen at Cuber reservoir, Black-winged Stilt and Kentish Plover chicks at S'Albufera, and even well into June there is still some passage and always the chance of late migrants such as Roller.

Return migration starts very early, with the best number and variety of waders passing through from late July and during August, when they are concentrated onto the few water-bodies that remain. Large flocks of Little Stints, Curlew Sandpipers and Dunlin, with smaller numbers of *Tringa* sandpipers, pass at this time, and scanning of these flocks has produced several rare waders in recent years. August also brings the first autumn tern movements, with ones and twos of marsh terns and even the occasional Caspian Tern. By mid-September some of the common summer visitors such as Short-toed Lark, Tawny Pipit and Woodchat Shrike have mostly departed but Eleonora's Falcon and even Bee-eater can be seen right through to late October.

In general, the autumn migration period is not so spectacular as in spring but the range of species to be found is surprisingly different. Passage continues right into early November when influxes of passerines can occur and Black Redstarts, White Wagtails, Song Thrushes and Robins fill the island. Some of the more sought-after species that regularly occur in autumn are Glossy Ibis, Spoonbill, White Stork and, later in the autumn, a few small groups of Common Cranes. Flocks of Greater Flamingos can appear at any time of year, but most frequently in autumn and early winter.

Clearly the above is only an outline of what species can be seen in Mallorca in the various seasons. As with any migration point, almost anything can turn up on Mallorca at any time of year, and year-round there is always the chance of finding rare or new species for the island.

Where to stay

We strongly advise the birdwatcher, with or without family, to base themselves in the north-east of the island, the towns of Puerto Pollensa, Alcudia and Puerto Alcudia being ideal locations within this area. This part of the island has many of the best birding spots close at hand, and many good beaches, hotels and facilities if accompanied by a non-birding family. The majority of travel companies can arrange packages to this end of the island, either in hotels or self-catering.

Should accommodation not be available in the north-east do not necessarily put off your visit, especially if the south is offered as an alternative, as this area has a good secondary concentration of sites, and one of the best spots on the island at Salinas de Levante. Staying in the south-west, the Palma/Palma Nova/Magaluf area, is to be avoided by the keen birder, as there are very few reasonable birding areas close by and access to the mountains is currently rather more difficult.

Food and shopping

Self-catering is becoming a popular option for birdwatchers as avoidance of hotel designated meal times allows greater flexibility when it comes to birdwatching. There has been an increase in the number of supermarkets and they are now easily found in all towns. Shops are usually open from 8.00 a.m.-1.00 p.m. and again from 4.00-8.00 or 8.30 p.m. so shopping should not interfere too much with birding, and all towns and villages are well supplied with good, cheap bars and restaurants. For those staying in Puerto Pollensa we can recommend Bar Llenaire, La Goleta, and Ca'n Toni/El Faro as excellent restaurants serving delicious local Mallorcan dishes as well as the usual international fare, all at very reasonable prices.

Getting around

Car hire is readily available and reasonably cheap throughout Mallorca, although it can be a little harder to find in mid-winter. Hiring a car throughout your stay is preferable, allowing maximum flexibility in relation to both the birds and the weather, but hiring for at least a couple of days is strongly recommended, allowing visits to the mountains and to the south of the island. Driving is easy on Mallorca (taking care to drive on the right, of course!), although some mountain roads are narrow and winding. Observe road signs and speed limits; the Guardia Civil is vigilant and can fine you on the spot. It should be stated here that random breath-testing is widely used on Mallorca. You need to carry your driving licence (the pink, European driving licences as issued in the U.K. nowadays) and passport with you when you drive. The wearing of seat belts is now compulsory at all times. Petrol is approximately the same price as in the U.K. and all major towns and holiday areas have petrol stations, most of which are open on Sundays and several are also open 24 hours a day. It is advisable to fill up with petrol before going into the mountains, as the only petrol stations are in Soller and on the mountain road that comes up from Inca, just before the junction with the C-710 (the main Soller-Pollensa road).

For those that cannot or do not want to drive, local bus transport is inexpensive and easy to use, and your holiday hotel or tourist information centre will have timetables. Bicycle hire is readily available in all the holiday areas, and bikes are especially useful for covering the Albufera and the lanes at the back of the Albufereta and Puerto Pollensa. Rather few sites are within easy walking distance of resort centres, although the Bocquer and Cala San Vicente valleys are walkable from Puerto Pollensa, and the northern and southern sections of S'Albufera are walkable from Puerto Alcudia and C'an Picafort, respectively.

Weather and clothing

The hot-and-sunny image of Mallorca presented by the glossy holiday brochures is by no means representative of the island's weather for much of the year. From June to early September it is invariably hot (over 30°C in the afternoon) and sunny, but it is also often very humid. Rainfall peaks in October, but can be heavy and persistant at any time from late September to December, and to a lesser extent through until May. Although the best times for birders to visit (April-May and September-October) are potentially the wettest, it is those same unsettled conditions that ground successive waves of migrant birds. Poor weather rarely lasts more than a few days on Mallorca, and is then followed by clearer, sunnier conditions which allows any grounded migrants to leave, before the next wave arrives. Thus in spring and autumn, the temperature can range from just a few degrees into the twenties, and the full range of clothing, from waterproofs, jumpers and boots to T-shirt and shorts, will certainly be required by the visiting birdwatcher. Snow can fall on the mountains from October to May, and anyone contemplating mountain-walking in mid-winter should be prepared for sub-zero temperatures.

Crime

Theft from tourist cars is unfortunately still regular on the island, and when hiring a car never leave any valuables in the vehicle unattended even for a short while: it is only inviting theft and the ensuing hassle that follows. Other forms of crime are rare, although of course petty-thieving and pick-pocketing can occur in tourist centres. These problems are best avoided by being sensible with valuables wherever you are, keeping your hotel rooms locked at all times, and making use of hotel safe facilities where available.

Other general points

The money unit is the peseta, now worth about 200 to the pound sterling. Places at which to exchange money, cash, travellers cheques, etc. ("cambio" in Spanish) abound in all tourist areas, and although hotels and many shops will also do exchange, the rates they offer are often slightly poorer than those found at banks.

The native language used on the island is Mallorquin (a dialect of Catalan) but Spanish (Castellano) is spoken by all islanders too, and in all the coastal holiday areas English will be understood, especially by shopkeepers (as will German, and occasionally French and Swedish). A phrase book is always a useful addition to the luggage.

At certain times of the year mosquitoes are in evidence, but they are rarely a significant problem, and should you react to bites it would be advisable to use suitable insect repellants when birding in the wetter habitats (notably S'Albufera and the Albufereta), particularly at dusk of course. The island has four species of snake but none of these are poisonous, and of the two species of scorpion only one stings, which is painful rather than dangerous. However, neither snakes nor scorpions are common anywhere, and they are very unlikely to be encountered.

The aim of this book is to guide the birdwatcher to the best birding spots on the island, but please bear in mind that details of sites, and in particular access arrangements, are regularly subject to change. Should "Privado", or any other signs that obviously mean no access, appear at a site previously described as having free access please take notice; failure to do so can lead to other sites closing up and thereby affecting all birders to the island in the future, as some previous, unfortunate, experiences have shown. The sign "Coto Privado de Caza" and the rectangular diagonally split white/black sign mean private hunting land and not "no entry" (unless of course accompanied by padlocks and other signs). Up-to-date access information is always available during your holiday at the birders indoor meetings.

Birders meetings, the GOB, and submitting records

Meetings are held at the Hotel Pollentia in Puerto Pollensa (see Map 3) every Monday and Friday in spring and autumn commencing at 9.00 p.m. and are run by the GOB/RSPB Representative. These meetings are free and are a friendly get-together for the exchange of bird and site information for visiting birdwatchers.

The local bird group is called GOB (Grup Balear d'Ornitologia i Defensa de la Naturalesa). From humble beginnings as a small bird club, GOB is now one of Spain's largest non-governmental conservation organisations, with the aims of conservation of the natural environment, increasing public awareness, and the study of the natural environment in the Balearics. All birdwatching visitors are able to help by forwarding their bird records to Graham Hearl, Apartado 83, Sa Pobla, Mallorca, for inclusion in the annual Mallorca Bird Report published in English. All these records are passed on to GOB, both for the record and when necessary for use in conservation campaigns. Records should be submitted in the form of an annotated checklist in Voous order (see the Mallorca checklist at the back of this book for guidance).

Using this guide

In some cases two names are given for the same place, due to the use of two languages in Mallorca. The principal name we have used is the one in current usage among visiting birders, but any regularly encountered alternatives are given in parentheses where relevant.

The scientific names of bird species mentioned in the text are given in the checklist at the back of this guide.

The system of numbers given in squares on several of the maps cross-references directly to the text for the relevant site, and the numbers are given in the text.

Most roads in Mallorca are marked on the roadside by Kilometre stones. These large, white stones with coloured tops show the road number and the number of kilometres to or from the reference-point town. Between these stones are small, all-white stones showing just a black number which split the kilometre into tenths. This distance labelling system is extremely useful for locating your precise position along a stretch of road, and we have used the Kilometre signs extensively in the text for giving directions. These values are given with a capital K, to the nearest tenth of one kilometre. Throughout the text, distances are given in kilometres, not miles.

We suggest that this guide is best used in conjunction with a good quality road map of Mallorca, of which there are currently several available from high street bookshops in the U.K. (the Hildebrand's TravelMap and the Firestone tourist map being examples).

For reference, Map 1 gives a general picture of Mallorca showing the airport, the location of the major towns, and of the best birding areas on the island as detailed in this Guide.

Map 1. The island of Mallorca, showing principal roads, towns and the birdwatching sites discussed in the text.

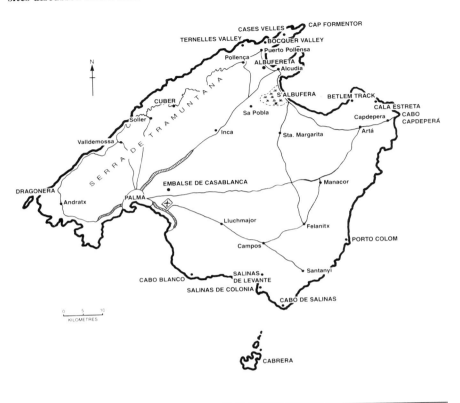

Birding sites in Mallorca

S'Albufera (Map 2)

The Parc Natural de S'Albufera de Mallorca, often known to British birders simply as the Albufera Marsh, is well-established as the best year-round birding site in the Balearic Islands, and is among the top wetland areas in the western Mediterranean. This is largely a consequence of the very active management of the Parc; indeed, some further changes will occur in the future, though none of these are likely to be as significant as those of the recent past, and one or two are anticipated below. An elevated view of much of the Parc is shown in Plate 1.

The main entrance to the Parc is at K27.0 on the Alcudia-Artá road (the C-712) on the south side of the "English Bridge" (S'Oberta). Many birders complain that there is no access to the Parc in the early mornings and late evenings, but this is only true for cars; there is *access by foot and bike at all times* through the gap in the wall on the south side of the main gate. In fact bicycle is the best way of getting around the Parc – there is a huge number of hire shops in Puerto Alcudia. Car access is from 9.00 a.m. to 5.00 p.m. in the winter and usually to 7.00 p.m. in summer. Note that on peak days in the spring and summer (often only Saturdays and Sundays), there is no car access. Unfortunately, this policy is a variable one, and for details of weekend access at these times of year, either ask in the Parc itself, or at the Monday and Friday birders meetings. If you should find the gates closed, it is possible to park safely in the gravel area about 100 m south of the main entrance on the landward side of the road, and walk from there.

The various options for routes once in the Parc are described, but it will become quickly apparent that there is no particular "best" order in which to visit the different parts of the Parc. Although the text separates the Parc into three sections, these boundaries are completely artificial and it is possible to spend a whole day combining all these areas, or visiting each on several half-day trips. Indeed, the fringe areas at "Orange Bridge", the waterworks and the Old Salinas are easily visited on-route to and from other sites, and many birders regularly drop in to one or other of these areas more or less every day to check for new migrant arrivals.

If entering or leaving the Parc through the main entrance, remember to check the artificial promontory at S'Oberta for loafing Audouin's Gulls (they are very regular in spring). The pine trees near the main gate are a favoured Night Heron roost. Evening is best for seeing these, ideally about half-an-hour before dusk, with over 60 regularly recorded in recent springs.

The central S'Albufera

Following the main track into the Parc, you arrive at the Reception area and car park after 1 km. Visitors should ideally report to Reception on arrival, though do not waste time waiting if it is unmanned. Reception should normally be open from 9.00 a.m.-1.00 p.m. and again from 2.00-5.00 p.m. Check the scrub around the car park for Serin, Sardinian and other warblers, and the trees for flycatchers and Golden Oriole. This area is also good for *Phylloscopus* warblers, especially Wood, but also Bonelli's.

From the car park area, there are several choices as to which direction you can go if on foot. Walking round behind the Reception building takes you over a small wooden bridge; here check the canal for possible Little Bittern. Go across the green metal sluice bridge, checking up and down the main canal for heron species (including roosting birds in the trees downstream), wildfowl and possible Purple Gallinule. Turning right after the green bridge takes you to the two Bishop hides (see Map 2).

A few hours in the Bishop I hide at any season is bound to be well-rewarded. Numbers of regular waders are good (shanks, Ruff, Black-tailed Godwit in spring, smaller waders when water levels are lower in summer) and this is one of the sites for Marsh Sandpiper in April. Any of the Parc's warblers may been seen from here, and the wide vista makes the area good for raptors, especially falcons and three species of harrier, especially Marsh, and also Hen in winter. Ospreys are often seen on the perching posts provided. The scrub around the hide is especially rich, housing Bluethroat and Penduline Tit in winter and early spring, and Cetti's Warblers year-round. Water levels tend to be less favourable at the Bishop II hide, but similar species are likely, and it is always worth checking.

Alternatively, head on the path that goes from the south-west corner of the car park through the trees towards the CIM hide. This hide overlooks a large, open pool which is good for wildfowl, Little and Cattle Egrets, possible Squacco Heron, and Black-winged Stilt and other waders. From this hide you can also see towards the open area beyond which often attracts Collared Pratincole in the spring. Whiskered and Black Terns are also possible in this area, especially after bad weather, when they may join the huge flocks of hirundines which gather over the pools – these hirundine flocks should obviously be checked for Red-rumped Swallow, any time from March onwards.

Coming out of the CIM hide, continue round on the track away from the car park until you come to a wooden bridge to your right. Going over this bridge will take you up to the view-point on the raised mound, and thereafter to the large stone bridge over the main

Map 2. The Albufera marsh, showing the adjacent dunes, waterworks and Old Salinas.

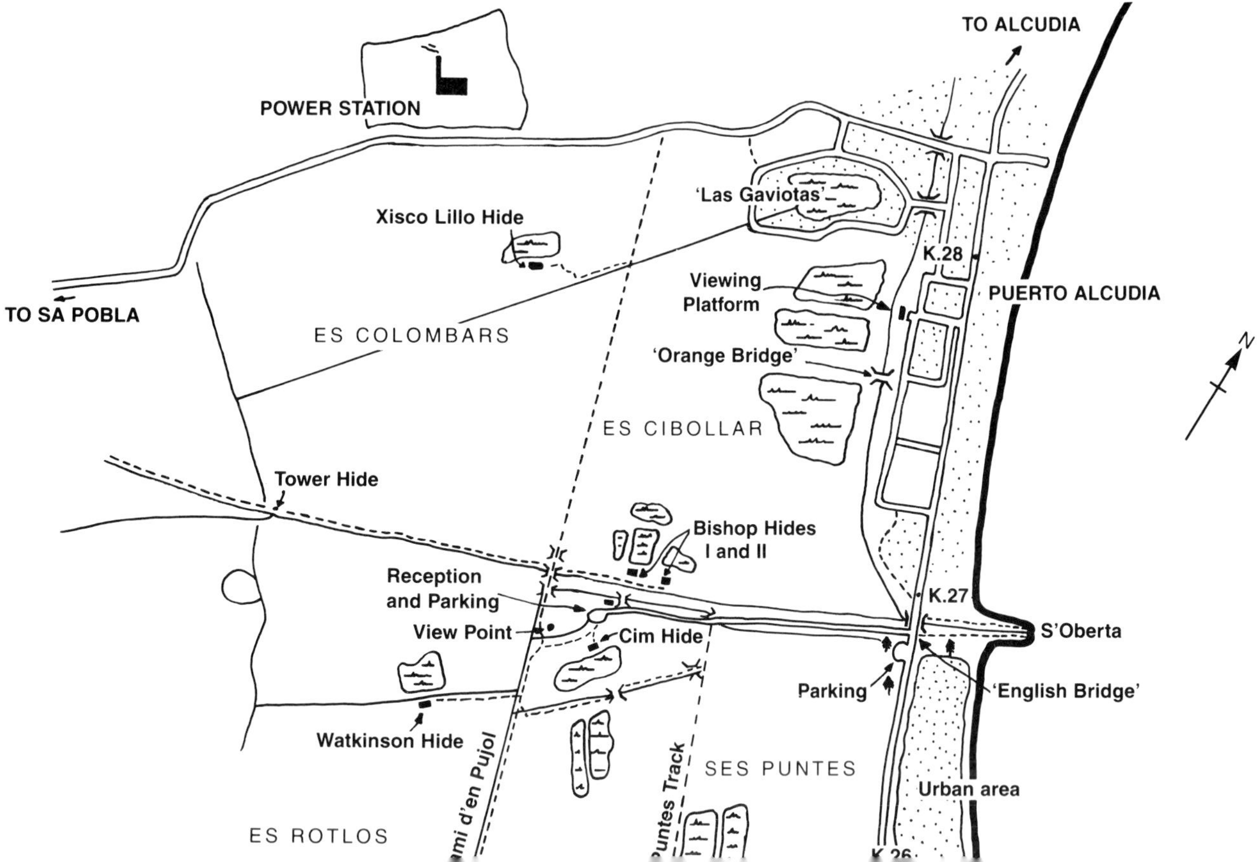

TO ALCUDIA

PUERTO ALCUDIA

S'Oberta

'English Bridge'

K.28

K.27

K.26

Urban area

'Las Gaviotas'

Viewing Platform

'Orange Bridge'

ES CIBOLLAR

Bishop Hides I and II

Parking

SES PUNTES

Puntes Track

Cim Hide

POWER STATION

Xisco Lillo Hide

ES COLOMBARS

Reception and Parking

View Point

Camí d'en Pujol

Watkinson Hide

ES ROTLOS

Tower Hide

TO SA POBLA

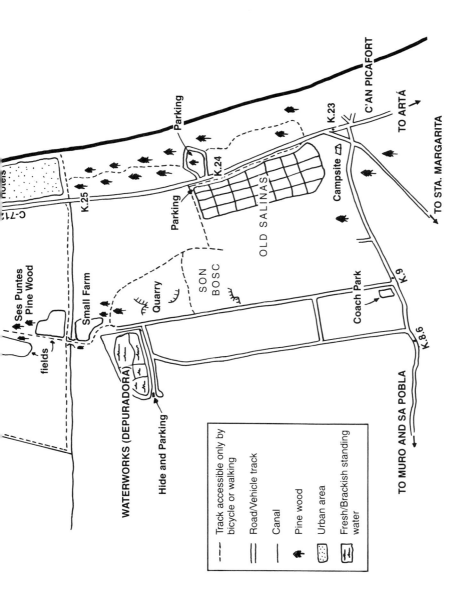

TO C'AN PICAFORT

Parking

K.24

K.25

C-71?

Hotels

OLD SALINAS

Parking

K.23

Campsite

TO ARTÁ

TO STA. MARGARITA

Ses Puntes
Pine Wood

Small Farm

fields

Quarry

SON
BOSC

Coach Park

K.9

K.8.6

WATERWORKS (DEPURADORA)

Hide and Parking

TO MURO AND SA POBLA

- - - Track accessible only by bicycle or walking

═ Road/Vehicle track

── Canal

🌲 Pine wood

▦ Urban area

▦ Fresh/Brackish standing water

11

canal. If you carry straight on, you can visit the Watkinson hide, reaching it by following the obvious markers provided throughout the Parc. In general, the water levels at the Watkinson hide are high, and apart from possible Purple Gallinule, you are unlikely to see species that cannot be found elsewhere. However, the opportunities for photographers are often good, with very close views of Little Grebe, Water Rail, Kingfisher and wildfowl. At present the other tracks that lead off from near the entrance track to the Watkinson hide, straight ahead down the Camí d'en Pujol, and to the left on the track that runs through the north of Es Ras, are both shut to the public. This situation is subject to change, and certainly if the Es Ras cross-track is open, it is well worth investigating. The typical habitat of this area is shown in Plate 2.

From the raised view-point, which offers an excellent view over the Parc, with good opportunities to see falcons and Marsh Harriers, walk northwards alongside the duck pond. This was built and stocked with pinioned duck for the education of local school children – so none of the duck on it are tickable! Continuing on the path, you very soon come to three consecutive stone bridges, the middle one of which crosses the main canal. Check up and down all the canals at this point for wildfowl, Little Bittern, Cetti's, Reed, Great Reed and Moustached Warblers, Penduline Tit in winter, and of course Purple Gallinule.

The stone bridge over the main canal is the best place to see the recently re-introduced Purple Gallinule. This former breeder was hunted to extinction early in this century, but was unlikely to recolonise naturally (which is now free from hunting) and so 29 birds from the Coto Doñana were released in August 1991 into this area of the Parc. The birds, marked with white plastic rings inscribed with three black digits, settled well, and have subsequently successfully bred with more birds being seen each year. There are perhaps 50-100 now in S'Albufera. Most birds seen now were bred in the Parc, but any observations of colour-ringed birds should be reported to Reception or at the birders meetings.

On the north bank of the main canal, you meet up with the track from the Bishop hides which is on your right. To the left there is a long track which runs alongside the main canal to the Tower hide, whilst straight ahead is a track running more or less due north to the Xisco Lillo hide.

The track to the Tower hide is noted for passerine migrants, Little Bittern and Purple Gallinule. The hide itself offers a superb view of the reserve. With patience, Little Bittern is guaranteed to give good views from late March onwards. Aerial feeders are best seen from here – if there is a suggestion of a hirundine passage, head for here, and look out for Red-rumped Swallow, Crag Martin (often hundreds in April), Pallid and Alpine Swifts in amongst the commoner species. Raptors are another speciality here – almost anything is possible, but this hide is famous as *the* Eleonora's Falcon watch-point. Some are usually visible any time from late April, but a record count of 102 (about 15% of the Balearic population) in a single flock in May 1992 was memorable. The track runs on past the Tower hide to the "Iron Bridge" (Pont de Ca'n Blau). This track is unlikely to yield much new in the way of different species, and is rather long, but can be used as an alternative entrance/exit for those with bicycles wanting to do a circular route.

Heading north from the main stone bridge for 1.1 km, you come to a turning on the left which takes you to the Xisco Lillo hide. Although comparatively recently erected, this hide now provides some excellent birdwatching, and again, good opportunities for photographers. This is the main loafing area for Cormorants (mainly present from September to April), is used as a pre-roosting area by Little and Cattle Egrets, and often attracts some wildfowl (with Marbled Teal a possibility in autumn/winter). Kingfisher and Moustached Warbler can often be seen very well from here, whilst the tamarisk scrub on the approach track is good for a variety of passerines, particularly Bluethroat. When the water level falls in summer, the hide can also be good for a variety of waders.

The final option in this central area of the Parc is the Ses Puntes track. The track starts from about midway along the entrance track, and runs off at a right angle from it, due south. In total, the track is nearly 2 km long, but although this makes for a longish walk, it is invariably worth it, with the whole area being interesting in almost any season. Walking (or cycling) back along the entrance track for about 400 m, you will see the Ses Puntes path on your right just where the main track bends sharp left over a bridge. Note that the Ses Puntes track is badly drained and is often quite wet, so wellies, or at least good walking boots, are recommended in all seasons except mid-summer.

After only a few metres of the start of the track, there are tall reeds growing on the right-hand side, and shorter reeds on the left. This area is excellent for Moustached Warbler, and early in the mornings, males can often be seen singing from high up in the shorter reeds. The grazed area to the left at this point is very good for herons and egrets, with Purple Heron particularly frequent, from late March to October. Other reedbed warblers are all likely to be seen well along this section of the track in the appropriate season.

About 200 m down on the right there is the other access point to the Es Ras cross-track, although as stated earlier, this is currently closed. Nevertheless, it is worth walking up onto the small bridge and checking the grazed pool complex (looking across to the CIM hide), again for herons and egrets, but also for wildfowl and waders such as Wood Sandpiper.

A few hundred metres further on, of course birding all the way, and regularly checking the skies for raptors, a series of large open pools will start to become visible on the left. There is a series of old gates along the path which afford reasonable views over these pools, and it is usually worth spending some time checking over this area. There are waders and wildfowl present in this area throughout the year, while marsh and Gull-billed Terns often appear here on passage, any heron or egret species is possible, and even storks and geese have been seen. These pools often attract huge flocks of hirundines in poorer weather, and tired, migrant swallows and martins often settle on the reeds near the path giving superb views: in these conditions, this can be excellent place to see Red-rumped Swallow. Just near the gate to the "Lone Pine" track, there is a set of steps by the wall on the opposite side of the track which take you up onto a wooden observation platform - this can be a good place from which to check these pools. The "Lone Pine" area – so-named by Eddie Watkinson, although there are now several trees – is a small area of raised, "fossil" sand-dunes. Unfortunately, the path across is nowadays almost invariably flooded, but in mid-summer it can be worth walking, in order to check the pools more closely, and for the excellent view from the top of the dunes.

Continuing on for another few hundred metres, you enter a small pine wood. Throughout this section of track, and around the wood, Woodchat Shrike is very likely (from April to September). The scrub and trees here provide excellent habitat for Sardinian Warbler, Nightingale, flycatchers, *Phylloscopus* warblers, Redstart, Serins and other finches. Although there are now warning signs about bees in the wood, it is extremely unlikely you will encounter any problems, and the area is often so good for migrants that it really deserves thorough checking. Beyond the wood there are fields which are good for pipits (including Red-throated), wagtails, Fan-tailed Warbler and Woodchat Shrike.

At the southern end of the Ses Puntes track, there are three options (in addition to returning) although two of these are currently poor. To the left, a track takes you out to the main road. Although there can be some interesting birding to be had along this track, it is at present very densely vegetated, and hard to walk down. The track to the right is really only worth taking if there is access back up the Camí d'en Pujol, turning this into a circular walk (currently, this Camí is shut). However, the track that heads to the south, towards the waterworks, is always passable. Although it is gated, there is no problem with going through here and past the small farm to the waterworks. The farm itself can be good for seeing larks and wagtails. The two small dogs here bark a lot, but are always chained.

NOTE: Bicycles can be very useful for covering the longer tracks in the centre of the Parc (those to the Tower hide, Xisco Lillo hide and Ses Puntes), but please note that several minor tracks cannot be passed by bike. These are the track that goes round to the CIM and Watkinson hides, and the green sluice bridge and Bishop hides track. It is possible to leave your bicycle safely at Reception and walk these areas. To take your bicycle round to the Tower and Xisco Lillo hides, go round Reception, over the wooden brige and then turn *left* on the broad track alonside the main canal – this will bring you to the large stone bridge.

The Depuradora and the Salinetes

The S'Albufera waterworks (or Depuradora) was built on the fringe of the Parc in 1990, and those of us who saw it being built were filled with a sense of anticipation – very few areas of Mallorca have deep, fresh water which maintains its level thoughout the year, and with relatively natural-looking banks (see Plate 4). We were not disappointed, and the site shot to fame as soon as April 1991, when Jon King found Spain's first Black-winged Pratincole there. Although it is no longer quite so good for waders, it is *the* site on the island for seeing gulls and terns, whilst its banks attract various passerines, mainly pipits and wagtails, swifts and swallows gather over it in huge numbers in passage seasons, and the view over the Parc is surprisingly good, making it an excellent area for seeing raptors.

Access to the Depuradora is by foot or bike from S'Albufera through the small farm at the end of the Ses Puntes track, or by car from the Sa Pobla/Muro road that comes off the main coast road at around K23. Coming south from Puerto Alcudia on the C-712, turn right before C'an Picafort at about K23.1, and then almost immediately right again towards Sa Pobla. After 1.0 km, turn right at K9.0 by the large coach depot onto the small straight road which leads straight to the Depuradora. If you miss this turn, or are coming from the Sa Pobla direction, you can alternatively turn at K8.6, onto another small road that again leads direct to the Depuradora (see Map 2). In both cases, turning left on reaching the waterworks takes you to a hide with a car parking area. The view from the hide is reasonable but it can be restricted: half-way along the south fence of the Depuradora, there is also a gateway which provides a good vantage point over the eastern pools, whilst at the pine trees nearby it is possible to get onto the low bank next to the track for a raised view over the hedge.

The Depuradora deserves several visits per week in migration times, and regular checking year-round. The loafing flock of Yellow-legged Gulls attracts rarer species, with Audouin's being regular in all seasons. Kentish and Little Ringed Plovers are resident, and it is the most predictable site to find rare waders (for Mallorca) such as Oystercatcher, Turnstone, Knot and Sanderling. Pratincoles favour the dry, gravel banks. Marsh terns are a real speciality here, and are possible at any time from April to September, but can gather in big, mixed flocks in late April and May – twenty each of Whiskered, Black and White-winged Black Terns, all in full summer plumage, is a truly impressive sight. This is also the best place for seeing Gull-billed and *Sterna* terns in Mallorca. The open vista from around the waterworks is excellent for seeing Marsh and other harriers, and Eleonora's Falcon, with always the possibility of other migrant raptors or soaring storks. Small numbers of wildfowl, sometimes rarities such as Ferruginous Duck or Common Scoter, can be found on the Depuradora's lagoons. The one or two White-headed Ducks you may see here (or possibly elsewhere in the Parc) originate from an (apparently failed) introduction scheme.

The rough habitat to the east of the Depuradora is an area of old quarry workings. This area formerly held a major colony of Bee-eaters, but now only half-a-dozen active nests remain, and these are more widely dispersed than previously. Nevertheless, this area is worth investigation, as you will stand a very good chance of seeing Bee-eater here in season, and Short-toed Lark, Hoopoe and many finches breed in the area. Beware that some of the north section of this site is now used for motorbike scrambling and should be avoided when in use. One path follows the Parc boundary from the big white house at the

Plate 1. The eastern section of S'Albufera viewed from the Puig de San Martí, with the Artá mountains in the far distance. The coastal dunes are visible to the left of the picture, and the "fossil dunes", with the Depuradora behind, to the right. The large brackish lakes of the Orange Bridge area are in the foreground.

Plate 2. A mixture of rush, grassland, shallow pools and reed, typical of some central areas of S'Albufera. The area shown, at the north of the Es Ras section of the Parc, has become well-known in recent years for regularly holding Red-throated Pipits in spring, while the pools can attract an excellent range of waders year-round.

Plate 3. *The Albufera is very heavily canalised, and the canal banks are typically lined with very tall reeds and in some areas with scrub and poplar trees. Such habitats are the best for seeing Little Bitterns and Cetti's Warblers, with Great Reed Warblers singing from the tall reeds in summer, and Penduline Tits often found in the poplars in winter.*

north-east corner of the Depuradora round towards the Old Salinas, whilst another cuts across the middle of Son Bosc; both are passable by bicycle, but car access is now prevented by a chain barrier at the Salinas end.

The Old Salinas (or Salinetes), situated alongside the C-712 road, are now also part of the Parc. Unfortunately, the lack of management between their abandonement in the 1970's and their recent acquisition by the Parc, has greatly reduced their value bird-wise. They can be viewed from various places along the tracks that run along their northern and eastern sides, and can produce any of the typical waders and wildfowl of the Parc, with terns or pratincoles in spring. They are at their best in July-August, when the low water level can make them one of the better areas for waders on autumn passage, and large flocks of Little Stints and Curlew Sandpipers occur on the middle pans, sometimes with rarer species mixed in. The single Mute Swans that can be seen here and at the Orange Bridge lagoons are escapes from a nearby collection.

The dune area, also owned by the Parc, at Es Comú (Plate 5) can be worth a visit if time permits, for Serin, Firecrest, Sardinian Warbler and Woodchat Shrike.

The "Orange Bridge" area

This area, officially known as the "Es Cibollar" section of the Parc, is named after the large, raised bridge on the eastern side of the main lagoons, which was painted a prominent orange in Eddie Watkinson's day. In this age of environmental awareness, it has been painted a rather more subdued green, but the name has well-and-truly stuck!

This area is a longish walk from the centre of the Parc, and is best accessed by car or bicycle off the main C-712 road using any of three or four short roads that run inland between K27.0 and K28.0. The northern pools are best viewed from the wooden observation platform (marked on Map 2), whilst the big, southern lagoon can be viewed from any point along the new road that runs alongside the canal.

The Orange Bridge area can be very productive all year round, with wildfowl, gulls, egrets and waders being attracted to the brackish pools in all seasons. A telescope is really a must for this site, especially as smaller waders tend to be found on the far side of the lagoons. This is the area favoured by wintering Great White Egrets, and can also be good for other long-legged species – Black-winged Stilt, storks, Spoonbill, Glossy Ibis and Greater Flamingo. The regular loafing flocks of Yellow-legged and Black-headed Gulls often attract rarer species, and Audouin's, Slender-billed and Mediterranean have all been seen. When the water level drops in the summer, more waders occur, and shanks and the larger sandpipers are regular.

Note that the large lake you will see marked on maps, to the north of the Orange Bridge area ("Lago Grande" or "Lago Esperanza"), is heavily disturbed and is extremely unlikely to yield any interesting birds.

The Albufereta and the "back roads" (Map 3)

This area is bounded by Puerto Pollensa to the north, Pollensa bay to the east, the main Alcudia-Palma road to the south and the Alcudia-Pollensa back road to the west. The whole area is one favoured by migrants for resting and feeding, and is always very productive for the birdwatcher prepared to spend time exploring the "back roads" and the Albufereta itself. Plate 6 shows a panoramic view of some of this area.

❶ Llenaire road. This road heads inland from the coast and is very good for harriers and Red-footed Falcon over the open fields during migration, especially in spring, and for Booted Eagle over the hills to the north. The fig and almond orchards before the

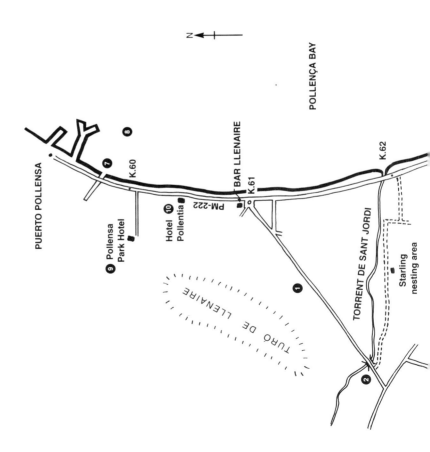

PUERTO POLLENSA

9 Pollensa
Park Hotel

7

K.60

8

Hotel **10**
Pollentia

PM-222

BAR LLENAIRE

K.61

N

POLLENÇA BAY

K.62

TURÓ DE LLENAIRE

1

TORRENT DE SANT JORDI

Starling
nesting area

2

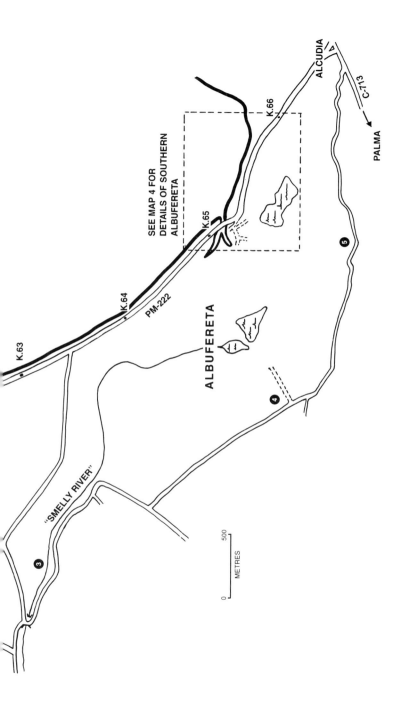

Map 3. The Albufereta and the "back roads" areas.

"Beehives" are a favoured spot for Hoopoe and, in spring, Golden Oriole; Roller has also been seen here.

To get there, follow the coast road (PM-222) until you come to Bar Llenaire on your right, at K61.0, turn right here and head inland down a road which commences as a wide road, then narrows when you come to the first open fields, proceed down the road, carefully looking on both sides, until you come to the "Beehives" area.

❷ The "Beehives". The area by the bridge now has only has one remaining beehive, but nonetheless is still a popular resting place for Bee-eaters on migration, especially in the evening. In spring, the almond orchards close by are good for Golden Oriole, while the bushes and vegetation by the *torrente* (stream) are good for warblers.

This area is reached by continuing down the Llenaire road until you come to a bridge over a torrente after 1.5 km. There is room for parking a few cars on the left by the track. It is possible to turn left here down this track (passable by car) that takes you back to the main coast road at K62.0; the fields either side and the Torrente San Jordi immediately north are also very productive in spring. It is in this area that Common Starling started breeding in 1993, and was joined in 1994 by a single Spotless.

❸ "Smelly River" (also known as "Nightingale road"). This road passes beside a torrente which sometimes smells badly, hence the name! Excellent for Nightingale, Bee-eater, Night Heron, Little Egret, sandpipers, passage migrants and some birds of prey in spring; Little Bittern and Squacco Heron have been seen.

Head south on the coast road out of Puerto Pollensa until you reach a turning on the right signposted "Pollença" at K63.5. Take this road for 2.3 km until reaching a sharp right-hand corner, at which point take the small turning to the left over a torrente, which is the Smelly River. Proceeding southwards along this small road, stop where and when you want for birdwatching – all around there is prime migrant habitat. Follow the road by the torrente until the road bears right, keep to the road for 500 m and take the first left – this road takes you around the back of the Albufereta (**❹** & **❺**) and eventually joins the main Alcudia-Palma road (C-713), where you can turn left and then left again after 100 m at the junction to return to Puerto Pollensa. This back road has various tracks off to the left, penetrating a little way into the marsh: explore where you fancy, bearing in mind that you may be on private land in places.

❹ View over middle lakes. There is a track here on the seaward side of the "back road", which leads up to a rise from which it is possible to view over the north lakes. Parking here is possible but not very easy, and is perhaps best covered by bicycle. Birds seen from here include Little Egret, Great White Egret in winter, marsh terns in spring and up to four Osprey.

❺ Here the back roads open to a view east over the main lake. This view point is ideal in the afternoon as the sun will now be behind you. It is an excellent area for Montagu's Harrier in spring, and the fields offer the usual passerines, notably wagtails and Short-toed Lark.

❻ Ca'n Cuarassa. This is an area much favoured by small falcons (notably Red-footed Falcon) and Woodchat Shrike, but is very sensitive to human disturbance, so please take notice of "Prohibido el paso" (no entry) signs and do not take cars in past the gravel parking area next to the restaurant.

To get there from Puerto Pollensa, head south on the PM-222 passing Bar Llenaire and continuing until you see the restaurant "Ca'n Cuarassa" on your right at about K62.5. Please bear in mind that the land off the main road is private.

❼ "Smelly stream". This small torrente is situated near the centre of Puerto Pollensa, on the coast road, in between Tolo's Bar and the Torre Playa/Bar Bistro. Especially in the early mornings and evenings this area can attract passage egrets, herons, hirundines and wagtails.

❽ Pollensa Bay and breakwaters. From outside the Hotel Pollentia it is well worth checking the breakwaters situated just offshore. They regularly have Shag (of the Mediterranean sub-species *desmarestii*), Cormorant and Sandwich Tern in winter, Yellow-legged Gull and invariably Audouin's Gull. If Audouin's Gulls are not here, anywhere on the beach between the town and the Albufereta is likely. The breakwaters have also produced the occasional rarity like Caspian Tern and Slender-billed Gull.

❾ Scrub behind the Pollensa Park Hotel. The area at the rear of the Pollensa Park Hotel is also worth an early morning look. It consists of scrubby vegetation, and can attract any passerine species. Typical birds are Sardinian Warbler, Goldfinch and Serin; migrants have included Great Reed Warbler, Subalpine Warbler and Ortolan Bunting. This area behind the hotel, the trees in front of reception and in fact any trees or power lines in the vicinity are excellent sites for seeing, as well as hearing, Scops Owl, especially in spring.

❿ The Hotel Pollentia. Venue of the Monday and Friday evening birders meetings in spring and autumn, and one of the more popular hotels for birders in Puerto Pollensa.

The southern Albufereta (Map 4)

This area of marsh surrounded by farmland is one of the most popular with birders, having easy access from Puerto Pollensa either by walking, cycling, bus or car. Access is gained from just south of the Torrente de Albufereta.

To reach the parking area at **❶**, head south out of Puerto Pollensa on the PM-222 road to the bridge over the Torrente de Albufereta at K65.1. Just past the bridge there is ample parking on the right hand side of the road by doubling back just in front of the small row of houses.

❷ Before proceeding down the track, first check the beach and small area of mudflats at the mouth of the torrente for gulls (Audouin's are often present), waders and occasionally terns.

❸ Walking inland on the track on the south side of the torrente, check the fields for pipits and wheatears, notably Black-eared in spring; Bluethroat is also possible in autumn or early spring. There is now a choice of route, either south down a side track to point **❼** or straight ahead to point **❹**

❹ Proceeding inland, pass over a small ditch (check for Green Sandpiper), and the track divides. To the left leads to a small stand of pines with a small finca (farm). Previously, we have enjoyed free access through this finca, but now a "privado" sign and a chain-link fence and gates have been erected: however a view of the main lake can still be had from this point. The area just before the pines resembles limestone pavement and is excellent for orchids in early spring.

❺ Proceed west of the pines, across the limestone pavement onto a well worn path – be careful to avoid treading on any orchids – and around the finca between two stone walls, on the path which leads to an obvious raised mound. From the mound, one can spend hours scanning all around. The lake can be good for Black-winged Stilt, herons, egrets, gulls, terns and waders. View west and north-west over the marsh for harriers, Eleonora's Falcon (in late April/May), Osprey and duck. Almost anything can turn up here – species such as Greater Flamingos, White and Black Stork, Glossy Ibis and Collared Pratincole have all been seen from here in recent years.

❻ Just down from the mound area facing south-west, you will see more fields. These fields and the mound itself are well worth checking for larks, pipits and finches; Red-throated Pipit has been recorded here, and Richard's Pipit has wintered since 1991.

Map 4. The southern Albufereta.

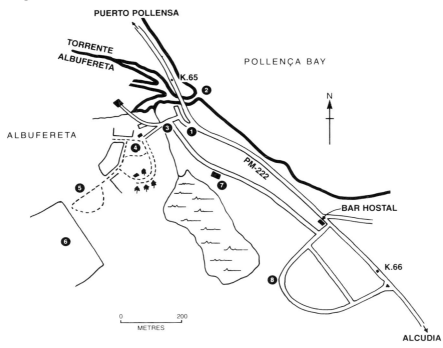

7 Returning to point **3** there is a track running south parallel to the sea. About 200 m down this track there is a derelict house on the right hand side – while this house remains derelict, the upstairs balcony makes a wonderful viewing platform for the lake, especially early morning with the sun behind you. Viewing from here gives you your best chance of seeing Tree Sparrow, a rare bird in Mallorca, but one which favours this corner of the Albufereta.

8 Carrying on down this track to the end and turning right brings you to a partly completed urbanisation. This area gives an alternative view over the Albufereta lake, again with good early morning viewing sunlit from behind. This area is excellent for Fan-tailed Warbler and, in winter, Bluethroat. This spot can also be reached direct from the main PM-222 road by turning inland at Bar Hostal (at about K65.6).

The northern valleys and the Formentor peninsula (Map 5)

This area, artificially named by us to facilitate ease of directions, is in fact the eastern extension of the main mountain range, the "Tramuntanas" (described later), and includes the area north of Pollensa and Puerto Pollensa, and the Formentor peninsula. These valleys are the main departure points for migrants in spring and a first landfall in autumn. Consequently, the bird populations of each valley in migration times are continually changing, even during the course of a single day. As well as being good for passerines, they are also excellent sites for watching raptor migration. The valleys and view points have been taken in order from west to east and not in order of importance.

Map 5. The northern valleys of Mallorca and the Formentor Peninsula.

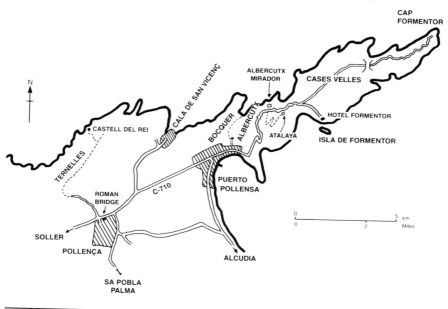

Ternelles Valley

Unfortunately this valley is now only open to the visiting public in spring from mid-March to early May, and again in the autumn, and even then only on Saturdays between 8.00 a.m. and 3.30 p.m. Entry is usually not allowed after 11.00 a.m. Parking is rather restricted along the approach road, so park where you can and walk up the valley (a nice walk in itself) until you reach the main gate where you must be signed in. It is a fairly long walk to the Castell del Rei but the views are stunning and the chances of seeing Black Vulture and Booted Eagle are very good. Also keep a sharp lookout for other birds of prey, Peregrine, kites and migrating Honey Buzzard. Other birds to be seen include Firecrest, Crossbills, and Wood and Bonelli's Warbler in spring. Plate 9 shows a view of the valley from the Castell del Rei.

To get to Ternelles, take the road out of Puerto Pollensa to Pollença, and pass the round-about at Pollença on the Soller road (C-710). After 0.8 km, the old Roman bridge is on the left, and at this point there is a minor road off to the right signposted "Ternelles 1.7 km". Take this road and park as far up as you can. It is probably wise to enquire for confirmation of access either at the birders meetings or at the tourist information in Puerto Pollensa, as the arrangements have changed several times in the last few years, and seem likely to continue doing so in the future.

Cala San Vicente

Not well-known as a birdwatching site, it would be very interesting to see what turns up in this valley with better coverage, as the area attracts its fair share of migrants, and is quite good for resident species too. The walk from Gommar over the saddle (Coll de Siller) to Cala San Vicente can produce the elusive Marmora's Warbler as well as finches and raptors.

To get there by car take the road out of Puerto Pollensa towards Pollensa until you reach a right turn signposted "Cala San Vincens" at K55.0. The walk over the saddle from Gommar is detailed in Mallorcan walking guides and most hotels have details of this popular local walk.

Bocquer Valley (Map 6)

Perhaps the most famous place name in Mallorcan birdwatching, the area is now somewhat changed from former times in that the almond orchards and olive groves at the base of the Bocquer have been partially developed, and the rough areas below the finca have been cut through by a network of roads for further urbanisation. Plate 10 shows the north ridge, frequented by a pair of Egyptian Vultures in recent years.

Access from Puerto Pollensa is very straightforward. Head east out of town on the road to Formentor. Where the road ceases to be one-way only, the Oro Playa supermarket is visible on the left, adjacent to which are the remains of a fine avenue of pines; this is the old entrance to the Finca Bocquer, and you will see the network of roads and the remaining olives and almonds. If walking, then proceed up the avenue of pines, or better still walk a winding route through the rough areas to the east of the pines ❶. Despite creeping development, the area at the entrance to the Bocquer is still a major collecting point for migrants in the right conditions. A walk round this area can produce Wheatear, Black-eared Wheatear, Redstart, Black Redstart, Wryneck, Hoopoe, Subalpine Warbler, Cirl Bunting and finches, and is a good place for raptor watching as it commands good views of birds drifting north-east along the mountain chain.

❷ From the avenue of pines, take the track straight ahead, on up to the finca itself. Half-way up the track you will be met with an imposing pair of gates. Do not be put off but open a gate, being careful to close it behind you, and continue on up to the farm – there is, at present, a right of way through the finca to the beach at the end of the valley. From the finca itself the view south-west is splendid. Be careful to check the trees on the terracing below the finca for birds – migrant warblers, Blue Rock Thrush, flycatchers and Hoopoe occur here. However, despite the view (shown in Plate 11) and the birds, try not to linger too long as you are right on the front terrace of the finca.

❸ At the entrance to the valley by the finca you will meet with another gate and maybe even a dog or two, but these are always on chains. Again do not be put off but continue through, and you are now in the Bocquer Valley itself. Follow the track through an impressive pair of rocks, birdwatching as you go of course; you will now see a small stand of pines lower down to your left: this is another good stop for raptor-watching (Plate 10). Then continue, if you want, right to the end of the valley. The view is worth it and it gives you more time to spot birds. Specialities of the Bocquer include Blue Rock Thrush, Cirl Bunting, Marmora's Warbler, Crag Martins most of the year, and Eleonora's Falcon from April to November along the rocky escarpment to the north-west. In addition, almost any migrant can turn up, and, as mentioned, Egyptian Vulture has been regular here in recent years.

❹ Returning to the base of the Bocquer and turning northeast along one of the new roads under the escarpment you come to "Postage stamp wood" on your right, and a small quarry a bit further on to your left. This entire area is all good birdwatching habitat, although more urbanisation has now taken the place of what was once pristine maquis and garigue. Nightingale, Pied and Spotted Flycatchers and various warblers can all be seen in Postage stamp wood in season (so named because of its rectangular shape). This area joins up with the next valley, the Albercutx.

Plate 4. The waterworks on the southern fringe of the Albufera, known as the Depuradora. Built as recently as 1990, this small site is already famous for attracting terns, gulls, waders and waterfowl, and as an excellent observation area for migrant raptors, herons and hirundines.

Plate 5. Coastal dune habitat, with areas of maquis scrub mixed with Aleppo Pine woodland, a habitat that is now highly fragmented in Mallorca. Characteristic species of these areas are Woodchat Shrike, Serin and Wryneck, whilst some sites still hold good densities of Marmora's Warbler.

Plate 6. *Pollensa bay from the Puig de San Martí. The Albufereta is visible in the middle distance, with Puerto Pollensa on the far side of the bay. The Formentor peninsula provides the backdrop, with, from left to right, the San Jordi, Bocquer, Albercutx and Cases Velles valleys all visible along its length.*

Plate 7. *Cases Velles viewed from the south-east. As the northernmost valley of Mallorca, large concentrations of migrants can be found here during passage periods. The area in the immediate foreground is one of the best on the island for Marmora's Warbler.*

Map 6. The Bocquer Valley and the "Postage Stamp Wood" area.

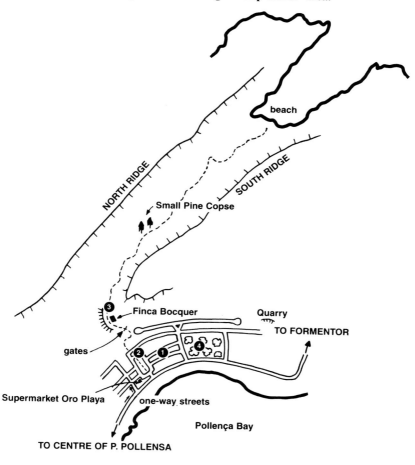

Albercutx Valley

Another good valley for migrants, once very popular with visiting birdwatchers. It is a little bit higher in the saddle with no exit to the sea. It is strictly private and entry is now totally forbidden; a look over the wall is of course advised.

Albertcutx Mirador and Atalaya

Not a valley, but recommended for raptor migration, Blue Rock Thrush, chats, wheatears, and, in winter, Alpine Accentor and even Snow Finch have been recorded.

The mirador is reached by continuing along the Formentor road, past the football field and on up to the top of the first ridge. Here you will see an obvious pull-in for cars and coaches at K5.2. Park here for the view and really close views of Crag Martin and maybe

Marmora's Warbler. The cliffs below hold a Pallid Swift colony, and these can be seen extremely well from here from May onwards. It is best to visit the mirador early in the morning before all the coaches arrive, as this is a popular tourist stop-off. Opposite the mirador there is a road that takes you to the top of the ridge and to the Atalaya, from where there is a magnificent view all around, and it is a splendid vantage point for raptor watching.

Cases Velles (Map 7)

Cases Velles (also known as Casas Veyas) is undoubtably one of the best areas on the whole of Mallorca for migrants in both spring and autumn. This importance as a migration site seems to result from its location as the northernmost cultivated area on the island, providing a last or first feeding area for birds in spring and autumn respectively. The main feature of this valley are the walled fig fields on either side of the road, shown in Plate 8. At times, when weather conditions are right, this area produces stunning migration effects with a constantly changing population of birds, even the same day.

To get there, follow the main road past the Albercutx Mirador, descending towards the Formentor Hotel and beach. At the foot of the descent take the sharp left turn signposted "Faro" (lighthouse). Continue on from this turning for 2.2 km through the pines until you reach the open area at K11.0. You are now at Cases Velles; park on the left just before the first field ❶, but if this is full try areas just past the fig fields on the edge of the pines.

❷ Scan the fig fields. These fields are private and access is not allowed, but this does not matter as viewing is good, and in fact the birds remain undisturbed, and so show well for those with patience. Check the fields from both ends for chats, wheatears and pipits including possibly Red-throated Pipit; in autumn 1990, an Olive-backed Pipit was recorded here (the first for Iberia). Check the trees for warblers, flycatchers (Collared has been recorded) and Turtle Dove. Don't forget to keep an eye on the sky for raptors, or the wires for Bee-eaters and, if you are lucky, a Roller. From this point, there is a choice of routes.

❸ Bearing in mind that there is no entry to all the enclosed fields, you are free to wander elsewhere in the woods, although it is certainly easier to keep to the footpaths. Walking south down the track by the edge of the fig field that is south of the road brings you to an old building with a very small field to the right. This field is used for general produce and always seems to have more than its fair share of seedy weeds: it is by far the best for finches and buntings, including regular Ortolan Bunting. Don't forget to look in the fig field to your left by the pig sty, it gives a different perspective from the view from the road and a closer view of the farther field.

❹ Continue the circular walk round, stopping at the water tank. Here Crossbills come down to drink, Firecrest and Serin should also be in evidence in the pines around, plus any other passerines needing a drink or bath. Golden Orioles often favour this smaller field at migration times. There are further viewpoints over the fields on the way round.

❺ At this point you can either continue round the fields by keeping to the left fork in the track to point ❻ looking for warblers, or fork right to point ❽.

❻ This point is a good area for trying to find Subalpine Warbler or Marmora's Warbler in the scrub and Bonelli's Warbler in the pines; Savi's Warbler has also been recorded in spring.

❼ Continuing round to where you rejoin the road brings you to the sheep wood. Unfortunately there is now no access into this wood, but it is easily viewed from the road and is a favourite spot for Hoopoe, thrushes and flycatchers.

❽ From either of points ❺ or ❻ you can take a more strenuous route to the right following a broad track that climbs up to the top of the ridge, from which you can see down the other side of the ridge to Pollença Bay and the Alcudia Peninsular. There is also a

Map 7. Cases Velles. The arrow symbols (⊢→) indicate the best available points from which to view fields.

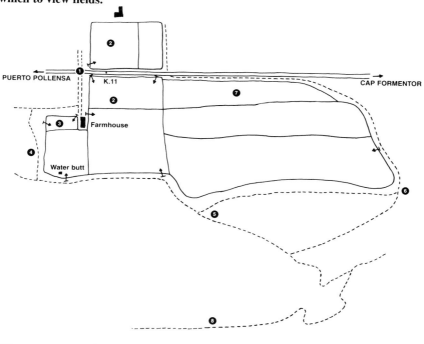

spectacular view of Cases Velles from here, as shown in Plate 7. The area around the track as it climbs up to the ridge, and particularly the top of the ridge itself, is one of the best on Mallorca for Marmora's Warbler. The best tactic is simply to sit and wait for them to appear – there are several pairs around the ridge-top. Peregrine and Raven should also appear while you are waiting, and keep an eye-out for other passing raptors, especially Osprey, Marsh Harrier and Honey Buzzard.

Due to its attractiveness for migrants, the turnover of species and numbers at Cases Velles is continuous in migration times. It is, therefore, well worth another look on the way back after a visit to the Formentor lighthouse to check on any changes in the birds later in the day.

Formentor lighthouse

Right at the end of the Formentor Peninsula you come to the lighthouse. It can be an excellent place for seeing Eleonora's Falcon when in residence from late April to the end of October; these falcons breed in late summer but are very often present on the breeding cliffs from May. The point can be good for sea-watching when conditions are right, although it is rather too elevated; a strong northerly is best when Cory's and Mediterranean Shearwaters can be seen offshore, plus any other large migrant or wanderer, perhaps Gannet or even storks. The pines below the light also hold migrants both in spring and autumn and Blue Rock Thrush is present all year, often around the car park. To get there, simply continue on from Cases Velles, stopping at any of the obvious viewpoints that take your fancy – Eleonora's Falcon can be seen from any of them, especially in autumn.

The Hotel Formentor area

The beach here is an ideal place to leave the non-birders in the family whilst birding Cases Velles, but beware of prices in the beach bars and even more so in the hotel; it is supposed to be one of the top hotels in Europe, and the prices reflect this. There are birds to be seen here in the surrounding pines – Firecrest, Crossbill and Chaffinch – and the small island offshore holds a recently-established colony of Audouin's Gull (seven pairs in 1992). The island also has Shag as well as dozens of pairs of Yellow-legged Gull, and all these species are reasonably visible from the mainland shore.

The Northern Mountains (La Serra de Tramuntana) (Map 8)

These limestone mountains form the dominant geological feature of Mallorca, rising to 1447 m (4748 feet) at Puig Mayor (higher than Ben Nevis), and running along the entire north coast of the island. Map 8 shows the central section from Soller to Pollença, the area of most interest for the birdwatcher. The high tops and surrounding areas provide excellent birdwatching, holding some of the most sought-after species on Mallorca: Black Vulture and Booted Eagle year-round; in summer, Eleonora's Falcon, Rock Thrush and Spectacled Warbler; and in winter Alpine Accentor and sometimes Snow Finch. A typical view of Puig Masanella, Mallorca's second highest peak, and its surrounding habitats, is shown in Plate 13.

Any of the excellent mountain walks detailed in June Parker's book "Walking in Mallorca" can be recommended for birding. Areas such as Puig Roig (now only open on Sundays) and the Mortitx valley (which may be closed halfway to the coast in the breeding season) are both excellent for Black Vulture and Marmora's Warbler. Note however that walks in parts of the mountain chain to the west of Soller are far less likely to produce birds of prey.

From the north-east of the island, the mountains are reached by taking the road out of Puerto Pollensa to Pollença, and passing Pollença on the C-710 road following signposts for Soller. There are various spectacular viewpoints and places to stop on the way up if you can find places to pull in. The obvious viewpoint past Escorca between K26.3 and K26.4 overlooking the Torrente de Pareis is well worth the stop if only for the view, but birds to be seen here include Rock Dove, Crag Martin and any of the raptors, particularly Booted Eagle and sometimes Black Vulture too.

The next obvious stop is at Embalse de Gorg Blau, the first reservoir just after the tunnel at K30.1. Crag and House Martins breed near the tunnel exit on the reservoir side. Stop at the various pull-ins by the reservoir looking out for Booted Eagle, Red Kite, Osprey and Black Vulture. When the water level is very low in late summer, Eleonora's Falcons come down to the water's edge to bathe. However, the most spectacular and productive mountain site to cover for birdwatching is Embalse de Cuber (Cuber Reservoir), so continue to K33.9.

Embalse de Cuber (Map 9)

❶ Park at K33.9 in the small car park, being careful not to block the access gates. There is another car park 100m up the road should this car park be full. Unfortunately, theft from cars is particularly prevalent at Cuber, so be warned.

Cuber is *the* raptor site in the mountains, and to see ten species in a single visit is not unusual: before you begin walking, always take an initial scan of the sky, and whilst you are at Cuber, keep half an eye on the sky at all times. The trip round Cuber can take from as little as one to over four hours, depending on your itinerary. Plate 12 shows a view over the reservoir from the south.

Map 8. The Serra de Tramuntana, the northern mountain range of Mallorca.

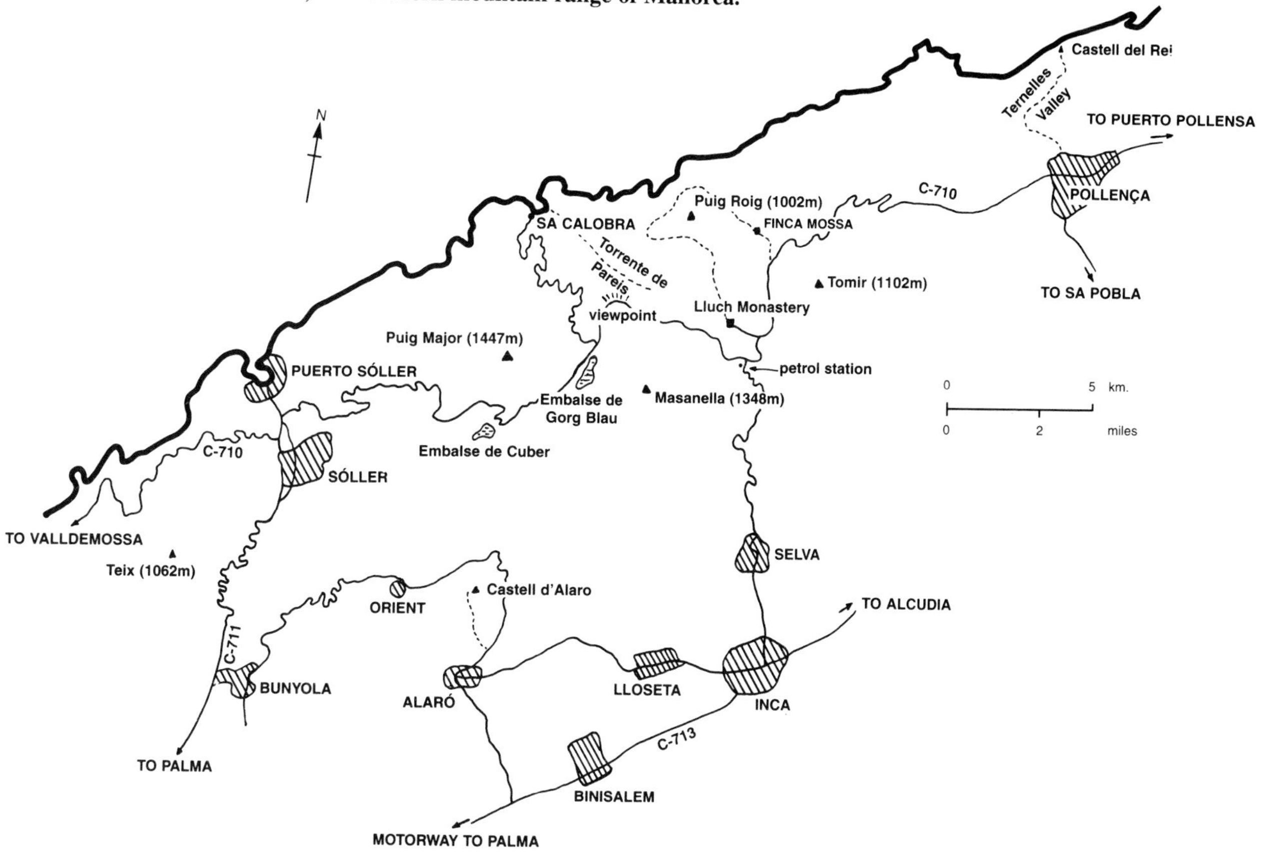

Castell del Rei

TO PUERTO POLLENSA

Ternelles Valley

POLLENÇA

TO SA POBLA

C-710

5 km.

2 miles

0

Tomir (1102m)

FINCA MOSSA

Puig Roig (1002m)

Lluch Monastery

petrol station

Masanella (1348m)

SA CALOBRA

Torrente de Pareis

viewpoint

Embalse de Gorg Blau

Embalse de Cuber

Puig Major (1447m)

SELVA

INCA

TO ALCUDIA

LLOSETA

C-713

BINISALEM

Castell d'Alaro

ALARÓ

ORIENT

MOTORWAY TO PALMA

PUERTO SÓLLER

SÓLLER

BUNYOLA

C-711

TO PALMA

C-710

Teix (1062m)

TO VALLDEMOSSA

N

Map 9. Cuber Reservoir, the premier birding site in the northern mountains.

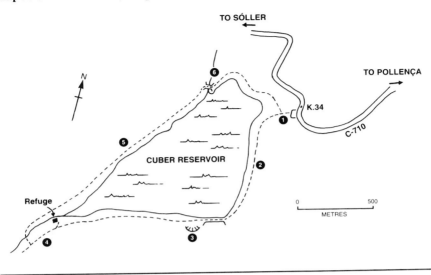

❷ Now you can take a slow amble round the reservoir, through the gate, heading straight on for the dam or branching off on the track to the right, as either direction can take you in a full circle around the reservoir.

Heading on the tarmac track towards the dam, the first birds you are likely to see are Stonechat and Tawny Pipit in spring, summer and autumn, plus Cirl Bunting and migrants such as Wheatear and Whinchat. Keep a lookout for Spectacled Warbler both sides of the track but especially in the scrub on the left after the first bend, and they can often be seen singing from the small pylons on the left. Wryneck can sometimes be heard calling from the scattered pines above the scrub, and the ridge here is good for Red Kite', Peregrine and Black Vulture.

❸ When you reach the dam scan the area below for warblers, Cirl Bunting and Serin; Moorhen has been seen here when there is enough water. The quarry just beyond the dam is a favourite place for Rock Thrush in summer, and the male can often be seen in aerial displays over the top of the quarry, from April to July.

❹ Following on round from the quarry, again looking for Spectacled Warbler, Rock Thrush and Tawny Pipit, you will see a refuge hut on your right hand side. This is a good place to stop for lunch as it gives you an all-round view of the mountains. Eleonora's Falcon often come to bathe around lunchtime from late spring to autumn, and this is as good a place as any to get close views.

❺ To return under the northern escarpment you can cross over a ladder-like stile by the refuge or you may have to return to the main track and continue on a little further, if the water level is high, to another ladder-like stile. Either way, you cross a tiny stream to get to the north side of the reservoir.

The north escarpment is very popular with soaring birds of prey, especially Booted Eagle, and anything can turn up here including the lone Griffon Vulture currently in residence on the island, or one of the 3-4 Egyptian Vultures on Mallorca. The scrub and rocks hold Blue Rock Thrush, Blackcap, *Phylloscopus* warblers and breeding Subalpine Warbler in a good year. Look out for Osprey on any of the pylons or on the shore of the reservoir, and Black Vulture over the ridge of Puig Major.

❻ The lower scrub and area of pools, when wet, are also good for Subalpine Warbler, Serin, Cirl Bunting, some migrants, and the omnipresent Sardinian Warbler.

Note: If you continue on the road towards Soller, the area between K35 and K36 is a military area – DO NOT STOP.

Castell d'Alaró and the Orient Valley

The ramble up to the Castell d'Alaró is a favourite itinerary for the walking tourist and the restaurant half way up can be recommended for the shoulder of lamb (Paletilla de Cordero). The Castell is signposted from Consell, on the main Palma road, and from Alaró; the road up eventually deteriorates to a rough track but is just passable in a hire car. It is possible to park at the restaurant and walk on up to the Castell – the views from the top are stunning, especially on a sunny day, and you have a good chance of spotting Booted Eagle and even Black Vulture flying below you.

Should you not wish to walk up to Castell d'Alaró, the road under the Castell through the impressive gorge to Orient is one of the best sites on the island for Booted Eagle.

The mountains to the west of Soller are little covered by visiting birdwatchers due in part to the distance from the Puerto Pollensa area. They are more wooded, and although Red Kite is more likely (especially between Santa Maria and Bunyola) any new information from here would be valuable. Why not explore, and report your sightings?

The Artá peninsula (Map 10)

The Artá peninsula, situated on the east side of the island, is a separate mountainous region, much lower than the Tramuntana range, but with a distinctive charm of its own. This region is especially popular with birders for Booted Eagle and Thekla Lark.

To get there from Puerto Pollensa go south on the coast road past Alcudia and on to Ca'n Picafort, and from there follow the C-712 coast road, signposted to Artá. Three separate itineraries for the Artá area are detailed here, but each one may need at least a half-day in itself, and it is not suggested that all should necessarily be attempted in one day.

❶ At K7.8 on the C-712, before Artá, there is a road to the left signposted to "Colonia Sant Pere". Take this road, keeping an eye open for Booted Eagle, until you come to Colonia Sant Pere, after 4.3 km. The road here bends to the left into the small resort, but continue straight on for another 4.5 km, at which point the road then deteriorates into a rough track. It is a good idea to park here – as usual, beware of thieving from cars here.

The fields along the first half of this road are interesting for Short-toed Lark, Woodchat Shrike, Cirl Bunting, Hoopoe and finches, and stopping off at any of the various pull-ins is likely to be rewarded.

❷ From the recommended parking point it is possible to continue straight on the track and walk for about 2.5 km under the escarpment in the direction of the Atalaya de Morei, birding all the way. Marmora's Warbler is common (although often hard to see) in the scrub below the escarpment, there is a small Alpine Swift colony in the cliffs high above the track from May, and always keep a lookout for Booted Eagle, Peregrine and other raptors above. For reasons that are not altogether clear, the coastal strip along this walk does rather well for migrants, with a wide range of warblers and flycatchers having been recorded here in season.

On the return either of the roads into Colonia Sant Pere can be taken to stop for a drink at one of the sea-front cafés: Audouin's Gull is regular along the coast here. You now have to return to the main road and continue the last 8 km to Artá, looking out from K7.0 onwards for Booted Eagle in the low hills all around the road.

Map 10. Birding areas in the Artá mountains.

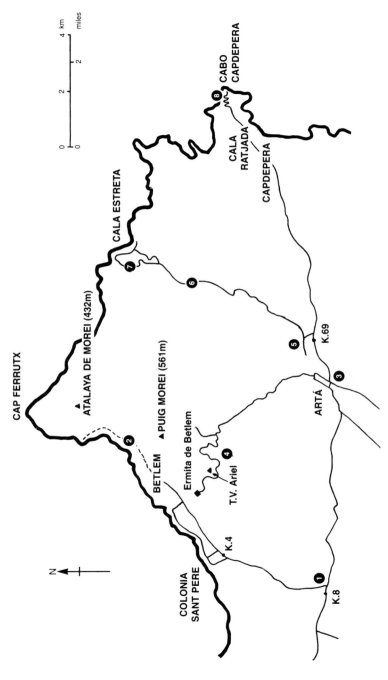

Plate 8. *Fields at Cases Velles. The mixture of grass fields, fig orchards, ploughed areas, scrub and pinewood adds to the diversity of species found here, and the site has a well-deserved reputation for attracting both local and national rarities.*

Plate 9. *Ternelles Valley, as seen from the Castell del Rei. Although best known for its migrant and resident raptors, and in particular as an excellent site for Black Vulture, other attractions include the many resident Cirl Buntings, and migrant passerines that favour the areas of mixed woodland, notably Bonelli's Warbler.*

Plate 10. *The Bocquer Valley. Being only a short walk from Puerto Pollensa, this site is perhaps the best known to many visiting birders. The north ridge, shown here, has been frequented by a pair of Egyptian Vultures in recent years.*

Plate 11. *The mouth of the Bocquer Valley, looking south. This view has changed out of all recognition in the last twenty years, with building encroaching ever closer to the valley. The fields and scrub in the foreground are often packed with migrants in spring, and Roller and Great Spotted Cuckoo have been recorded here in recent years.*

3 Artá Town. To cover the remaining sites on the Artá peninsula, you need to know two routes through Artá town itself.

(a) To Ermita de Betlem. At Artá, take the first right signposted "Cala Ratjada, Capdepera, Manacor, Palma"; at the T-junction at the end, turn left signposted "Capdepera, Cala Ratjada"; after 50m, on a bend, turn left signposted "centre/centro"; go straight on this road into Artá past a church on the right until you come to a T-junction (after 500 m); a sign in front says "Capdepera" to the right and to the left, a pink sign "Sant Salvador, Museu, Ermita". Turn left, go past a small square and take the first right, again pink signs for "Ermita, Sant Salvador" (this turn, 150m after the square, is small and tight, so be careful not to miss it). Follow this road out of the town passing the cathedral Sant Salvador on your right. There is a black sign saying "Ermita de Betlem 9" and you are now on the Ermita road on the way to one of the best areas in Mallorca for Thekla Larks.

At K1.3 the road forks, take the left fork still signposted Ermita. At K4.7 the road forks again, again bear left (the right fork goes to a quarry and eventually the tall communications tower but access is never guaranteed, the track is bad and these days there are better spots around Artá for birds). The road now narrows and starts to climb, with the views getting more and more impressive.

4 Approaching the top of the ridge, at K7.0, there is a small communications tower on the right, and just after this, park on the right at K7.2. You are now in prime Thekla Lark territory, and both Tawny Pipit and Booted Eagle are also likely.

A further 50 m up the road on the left-hand side a narrow track has been bulldozed through for access to a small reservoir. This track is now gated but access on foot is possible and we recommend the short walk to where the track overlooks this reservoir. The habitat through which this track passes is excellent for Thekla Lark. In late autumn and winter Chough and Alpine Accentor have been recorded around the reservoir.

Back at the car, you can return to Artá, or continue down the last 2 km to the Ermita itself. Parking outside the Ermita gate, follow the track on the right, signposted "Fuente/Font", round past the small fields and onto the small headland. The fields in this tiny valley hold Cirl Bunting, Blue Rock Thrush, migrant finches and thrushes, and Thekla Lark in autumn. The pines here are excellent for Firecrest. Thekla Lark, wheatears and chats frequent the small headland, which affords stunning views over Alcudia Bay to the Formentor Peninsula beyond.

To get back through Artá returning from the Ermita, aim to retrace the entrance route. You will find that due to the one-way system this is not quite possible. Nevertheless, following the one-way system quickly brings you onto the main Cala Ratjada road, but with the road to the town centre about 100 m to the right. From here you can turn left for the Cala Estreta/Cala Torta sites described below, or right to return to Puerto Pollensa.

(b) Cala Estreta, Sa Cova and Cala Torta.

From the left at the junction signposted "Capdepera, Cala Ratjada", instead of turning left into the town centre, continue on through the town for about 1.0 km. Approaching the first main bend out of the town, there is a crossroads sign, and turn left towards "Cala Torta, Depuradora"; there is a beige building with large russet doors in front of you on the right side of the road, "Parc Artá", which is the fire station.

5 At a T-junction 200 m further on, turn right. Immediately on your left is a small depuradora (water treatment works), which can be worth a look if only for the wagtails, but a Sacred Ibis (presumed escaped from captivity) was seen here in 1990. Following this road eventually brings you to the coast. Note that the road is in bad repair with large potholes in places, but should be easily passable in a hire car. About 3 km from the T-junction, there is an impressive escarpment on your right, much favoured by Booted Eagle.

❻ A further 3 km will bring you to a spectacular viewpoint, giving excellent views of Crag Martins right below you. Around the rocky areas preceding this viewpoint, Rock Thrush bred in 1992 and may still do so; Peregrine is also regular here. Descending from the viewpoint for about 3 km you reach a pair of gates with a rustic sign on the left depicting rubbish, with an arrow to the right to Cala Torta, but ignore this and go through the gates. This area was designated for development, but for now it is a marvellous wild area. Just through the gates the road forks – it does not matter which route you take as this part of the road is a circular route, but the left one takes you more directly to Cala Estreta at the coast.

❼ The coastal scrub area is excellent for Thekla Lark, Tawny Pipit, scrub warblers, and the sea can provide views of shearwaters, Shags and gulls, often including Audouin's Gull. Just to the north offshore is a small islet with a colony of Common and Pallid Swifts in season. To return, just follow the road round back to the rustic signpost.

❽ Cabo Capdepera. This small headland is poorly known and may be worth a look if time permits. It is not ideal for seawatching but shearwaters should be seen, and visible migration of wagtails and pipits, and some scarce seabirds, has been recorded.

Southern Mallorca (Map 11)

The general area of the Salinas and Cabo de Salinas in the south of the island is shown in Map 11. In the absence of mountains, the southern part of Mallorca has a significantly drier climate than the rest of the island, and coupled with a flat relief, has many more Stone Curlew and larks than elsewhere. The S'Avall estate, which covers a large area of the cape, is privately owned and entry is strictly forbidden at all times. Annoying as this may be to birdwatchers it does mean that there is a large tract of pristine maquis and garigue and two large lakes undisturbed by tourists – ideal for the local fauna and flora.

The town of Ses Salines is marked and it is worth mentioning here that a very reasonably priced, good quality "menú del día" is available at the Bar Cana in the middle of the town, on the left when approaching from the Salinas de Levante direction.

To get to this superb area from Puerto Pollensa take the coast road south to Alcudia and the C-712 to Ca'n Picafort. Just before Ca'n Picafort by the camp site (at K23.1), take the right fork signposted "Santa Margalida". From there follow signs to Manacor by-passing Petra; it is possible to cut through Petra across country following signposts to Felanitx but the simpler route is via Manacor. At Manacor follow signs to Felanitx on the C-714 and then turning right in the town, on to Campos. Just outside Campos on the C-717 road to Santanyi turn right on the road to Colonia San Jordi. After 7.5 km on this road you come to a crossroads: here turn left to Ses Salines, right to Cabo Blanco, or carry straight across for the Salinas de Levante (see Map 11). One kilometre from the crossroads, there is a sign on the right for "Banys de la Font Santa"; pull in by this sign on the access road to the Banys (salt baths) and park: you are now at the start of the Salinas de Levante.

Salinas de Levante (Map 12)

The Salinas de Levante (known locally as Salobrar de Campos or simply Salobrar) is a large area of active and disused salt pans which attract a wide variety of migrant waders, wintering duck, small flocks of wintering Flamingo and Common Crane in most years, as well as holding a breeding colony of over one hundred pairs of Black-winged Stilt. Plate 14 shows a view over these salt pans.

It must be stressed that there is no access onto or around the pans and there are large, multi-language signs to this effect. This lack of access and, therefore, lack of disturbance (except for sporadic shooting around the edges in winter) is again very beneficial to the birds. There are two means of covering the pans, a track that cuts across the northern

Map 11. Birding sites in southern Mallorca.

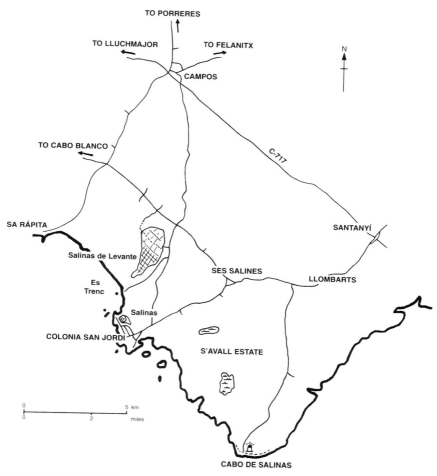

disused pans known affectionately as "Eddie's Track" (after Eddie Watkinson who first discovered the birding potential of this walk), and the access road to Es Trenc beach which passes down the east side of the worked pans. Both alternatives give excellent views of any birds present in the area, and combining the two gives very comprehensive coverage of the site. Year-round, and especially in migration seasons, the Salinas deserve at least a half-day's birding.

❶ Having parked at the side of the Banys approach road, first scan over the pans, which are disused at this northern end, for Flamingos in spring, autumn and winter; you are also likely to see Marsh Harrier and Osprey. Walk towards the Banys and turn right down a track towards three big palm trees, scanning the fields on either side for larks, whilst listening out for Quail. This is "Eddie's Track".

❷ At the first left hand corner of the track look over the lake in front of you. When the water level is quite high this is especially good for the larger long-legged waders including

39

Marsh Sandpiper in spring. When the water level is lower, Little Stint and *Charadrius* plovers will be seen.

3 Continue left down the track. The first right hand bend can be very muddy and sometimes impassable without wellington boots especially after heavy rain, but it is well worth struggling through as the birding gets better and better.

There are now disused pools, with varying depths of water, on both sides of the track.

Map 12. The Salinas de Levante (also known as Salobrar de Campos).

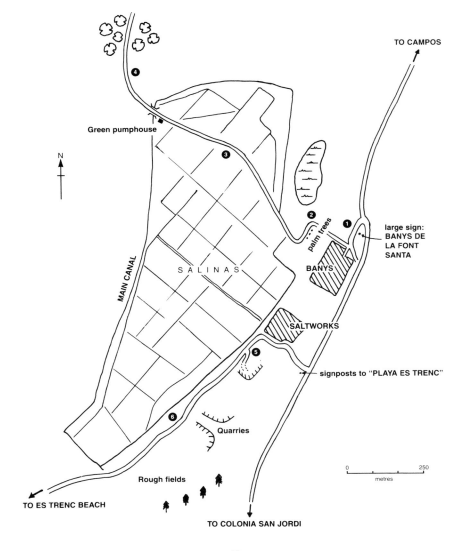

These pools hold a diverse range and number of waders depending on water-depth and time of year; regular species in the appropriate season include Marsh Sandpiper, Temminck's Stint, Wood Sandpiper, Spoonbill, Curlew Sandpiper and Curlew, as well as many of the commoner waders: Kentish, Ringed and Little Ringed Plovers, Little Stint, Dunlin, and of course Black-winged Stilt. Storks and Spoonbill have also been recorded. Stop halfway along at the white, square concrete building with two small windows – the pans on either side of the building are usually the best for birds and Flamingos certainly favour this area.

❹ Continuing along the track you come to a green pumphouse, at the end of the pans. If time permits it may be worth following the track beyond to the scrub area for warblers and to the fields further round which are good for larks and Montagu's Harrier on migration. Otherwise, return along Eddie's track to the car.

❺ Returning to the car, continue down the road towards Colonia San Jordi for about 400 m – the first main turning on the right is signposted "Es Trenc", turn here and drive past the salt works. Just past the sharp left hand bend there is a small raised access track to a small sand quarry, and it is possible to park up here (being careful not to block access). The view from here is probably the best point for scanning the active pans for the smaller waders as well as for Flamingos to the back and south, not forgetting to look for wagtails, pipits and other passerines on the margins. Terns (especially Gull-billed and marsh terns) and gulls also need to be looked for, and on one memorable occasion the pans were covered with several thousand Black Terns on migration. The quarry at your back is worth checking for Stone Curlew and Short-toed Lark but be careful not to disturb nesting Kentish and Little Ringed Plover in the breeding season.

❻ It is well worth checking further along this road, as pratincoles particularly favour the causeways between the southern pans, whilst Bee-eaters have been known to nest in the small quarries by the road. Parking is now more difficult as the farmers have been blocking up the more obvious parking spots, but pull in to any suitable lay-by, being careful not to block access.

This road continues down to Es Trenc beach. The road is fenced and there is a paying car park at the end which may be shut on weekdays out of season, but the beach can be worth a look, especially if the weather is poor, for seabirds and passage wildfowl.

Colonia San Jordi

Returning to the main road (see Map 10) continue towards Colonia San Jordi where there are some more salinas. As you enter the town there is a "Repsol" petrol station on a fork, at which you keep right. After 550 m, take the seventh turning on the right (other turnings to the right around this point will also suffice). The salinas are straight ahead of you, and are reached after 450 m. These salinas are much smaller than the Salinas de Levante but are worth checking and can be easily viewed from the road. The area is under-watched but would probably prove very productive if covered in the early morning. Superb views of Audouin's Gull are virtually guaranteed here, with sometimes over 20 present at one time, whilst Slender-billed Gull has been recorded here in all seasons. A good range of waders has also occurred here, especially in summer as the pans dry out. The surrounding scrubby area is good for warblers, and Dartford Warbler has been seen in winter.

Note that the left fork by the petrol station as you enter the town takes you to the harbour where the boat leaves for Cabrera.

Cabo de Salinas

This is the most southerly point of Mallorca. It is a most marvellous area of pristine maquis and garigue that has not been developed, and it will very probably remain that way as the land either side of the approach road is owned by the S'Avall estate. There is a splendid view of the Cabrera archipelago to the south and this headland is the best sea-watching point in Mallorca, offering an excellent chance to see Cory's and Mediterranean Shearwaters from land. Terns, skuas, and Gannets have also been recorded, whilst Audouin's Gulls pass-by regularly or loaf on the rocks near the lighthouse. A good tip is to watch for fishing boats that are gutting fish; apart from gulls, Cory's Shearwater and Mediterranean Shearwater sometimes follow boats for discarded offal.

An hour or two at the Cabo is easily combined with the morning at the Salinas de Levante. To get there from Colonia San Jordi, follow the main road towards Santanyi to Ses Salines (if coming from the Salinas de Levante, return towards Campos and at the first crossroads, turn right to Ses Salines) (see Map 11). From Ses Salines going east towards Santanyi, take the first right turn after 2 km signposted "Far des Cap Salines" – the sign is the small brown type. This turning is on the first left-hand bend after the big "Botanicactus" garden centre. If you get to the small village, Llombarts, you have gone too far.

This road leads direct to the Cabo and it is well worth stopping at various viewing points over the surrounding fields and scrub along the road. Popular stops are at K1.5; from K5.0 onwards, especially K5.5; and between K6.6-K6.8, especially at K6.7. Species possible throughout this area are Stone Curlew, Red-legged Partridge, Thekla Lark, Short-toed Lark and any passing harriers or Booted Eagles. There are high walls in places along the road, notably around K5-K6, so either view from gates and entrances, or from the top by climbing up the stone ladders built into the walls themselves.

Continue on to the lighthouse where there is reasonable car parking either side of the road, but again be careful not to leave anything of value in the car. The lighthouse garden can be worth a quick check from over the wall – Bar-tailed Desert Lark (the second for Iberia) was found here in March 1994, but expect the more usual larks and scrubland passerines.

Passing by the lighthouse garden to the sea there is now a choice of routes – you can turn right along the coast but the hinterland is fenced and very private, so it is best to turn left through a breach in the stone wall between the lighthouse and the sea. For seawatching, sitting on the leeward side of this wall, or on the rocks below the lighthouse, is the best spot. Walking below the lighthouse over the rocks, a rough path brings you to a marvellous area of maquis with good level paths along the coast and it is possible to wander slightly inland and cover the open areas for Stone Curlew and Red-legged Partridge. Another speciality of the area is Marmora's Warbler, which favours the coastal scrub. This whole area can provide spectacular signs of migration in autumn, with parties of hirundines constantly passing overhead, occasional large parties of Bee-eaters, plus the odd raptor or two deciding to continue the journey south.

Porto Colom (Map 13)

A town with a large, natural, enclosed harbour, but the birdwatching interest is centred on the small peninsula between the harbour and the sea. The habitat here is garigue, the scrubby vegetation typical of Sardinian and Marmora's Warblers, with Thekla Lark in more open areas. However, the whole peninsula is under threat, and has been developed from the lighthouse, spreading north and westwards at an alarming rate, and there is evidence of more to come. Nevertheless, at present Porto Colom is very worthwhile visiting, as an excellent area for both migrant and resident species.

To get there from the Puerto Pollensa area follow the route through to Felanitx. Approaching Felanitx turn left at the first roundabout signposted "Porto Colom". Following this road for about 12 km, you enter Porto Colom. Here, take the first turning on the

Map 13. Porto Colom.

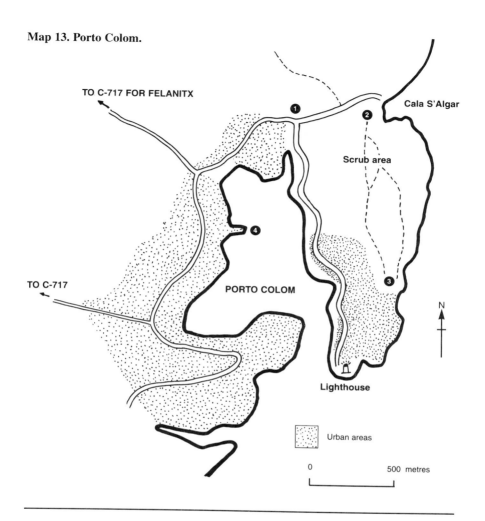

TO C-717 FOR FELANITX

Cala S'Algar

Scrub area

PORTO COLOM

TO C-717

Lighthouse

N

Urban areas

0   500 metres

left towards Cala S'Algar signposted "Sa Punta, far" (the word far means lighthouse in Mallorquin) – the end of the harbour will be on your right. Follow this road up through a small section of the town, going straight through until you descend a hill and the road opens out, with fields on your left and the harbour again on your right.

❶ The road bends sharp right towards the lighthouse, and on this bend a gravel track leads off to the left and to Cala S'Algar (not signposted). Take this track, but stop near its start to look at the wet fields to the north. These can be very good for gulls and waders in passage periods.

❷ Follow the track round to the Cala and park in one of the obvious pull-ins. The fields and headland to the north are very good for larks, wagtails and wheatears during migration. Having checked this area, walk south up the slope and through the scrub to the fringe of the new development for Marmora's Warbler, Thekla Lark and Tawny Pipit as well as migrants, and Dartford Warbler in winter. The path along the cliff edge is good for Stone Curlew, Pallid Swift and wheatears.

3 Working south along the coast path, just at the start of the newest development, you come to a small bay and sea cave. This is the main Pallid Swift colony and is also an excellent area for Blue Rock Thrush. Sea-watching from the coast can also produce shearwaters, while Audouin's Gulls regularly fly past. The development between here and the lighthouse is worth checking as Rock Sparrow bred around here in 1994, and Trumpeter Finch has been recorded in this area recently.

4 The harbour is well worth a look, not only for Shags and Audouin's Gull but also for migrant terns, with both Black and Gull-billed having been recorded.

Cabrera (Map 14)

When founded in 1991, the archipelago of Cabrera, off the southern tip of Mallorca, became the first National Park in the Balearic Islands, and the first joint maritime-terrestrial Park in Spain. This is wholly justified recognition of what is a truly superb area for both wildlife and scenery. Ornithologically, the quality of the islands has long been recognised. Cabrera holds very important colonies of Audouin's Gull, Cory's and Mediterranean Shearwaters (of the endemic race *mauretanicus*), Storm Petrel, Shag and Eleonora's Falcon, as well as breeding Peregrine and Osprey. However, since the creation of the National Park, intensive research undertaken largely by GOB has demonstrated Cabrera to be a very important site for observations of passage migrants. Access conditions are subject to change, and it is only possible to walk over a limited area of the main island. Nevertheless, it is well worth a visit, and in any passage season the main valley (illustrated in Plate 15) can be packed with passerine migrants.

Cabrera is currently served with a daily boat trip from 1st April to 30th September starting at 9.30 a.m. from Colonia Sant Jordi, and returning at 5.30 p.m. (rarely, the boat may go to and from Porto Petro). The price quoted for 1995 is 2700 pesetas per person. Food must be taken, as there is none available on the boat or on the island, although drinks can be bought on both. It is advisable to book places on the boat trips in advance at all times, and this is essential both early in the season when trips may be cancelled due to the weather, and later in the summer months when the trips are very popular. The maximum party size that can be covered by a single booking is 20, although it may be possible to negotiate access for larger groups. The telephone number for bookings is (00-34-71) 649034. The trip goes to or around Cabrera and lands at the harbour for a few hours.

The boat journey across from Mallorca to Cabrera affords excellent views of the two shearwaters, often as the boat passes near or even through large mixed rafts of loafing birds. Shags are guaranteed, and Audouin's Gulls will be seen near islets and in the main harbour. From the boat or on land, Osprey, Peregrine and Eleonora's Falcon (the latter from late April to November) should also be seen. When landing at the small port, you will see a valley to the south at the far end of the harbour (see Map 14). That is the best area for seeing migrant passerines. However, it is important to clarify with the Park staff where you can walk, as there is often restricted access into the valley. All the scrub around the harbour and up the valley contains Marmora's Warblers, and there are several pairs of Subalpine Warbler, Cabrera being the most important breeding site for this species in Mallorca. At the very least walk around the harbour to the fields at the foot of the valley, but if possible, arrange to walk up to the monument to the French soldiers, part-way up the valley. During migration, the fields can contain an abundance of larks, pipits, wagtails, buntings, chats, starts and wheatears, whilst the bushes are alive with warblers and flycatchers. In addition to all the commoner migrants, Cabrera is an excellent place for Ortolan Bunting, Golden Oriole, Black-eared Wheatear and *Hippolais* warblers, whilst rarities such as Spanish Sparrow, Rufous Bush Chat and Collared Flycatcher have been more or less annual in recent years.

Plate 12. Cuber Reservoir viewed from the south. Puig Major, Mallorca's highest mountain at 1447 m, provides a stunning backdrop, the effect being only slightly spoilt by the military installation at its peak. The reservoir is the most accessible breeding area for Rock Thrush and Spectacled Warbler, and ten or more species of raptor can be seen here in a day.

Plate 13. Puig Masanella, the second highest mountain in Mallorca. The habitats in the foreground, extensive Evergreen Oak forests with small agricultural plots in the valley bottoms, are typical throughout the northern sierra, and abound with Nightingales, Cirl Buntings and Serins. The mountain peak itself is an excellent site for Alpine Accentors in winter.

Plate 14. *Salinas de Levante (Salobrar de Campos). A mixture of active and disused salt pans, this area attracts a wide diversity of migrant waders, and has over one hundred pairs of nesting Black-winged Stilts.*

Plate 15. *The main valley of Cabrera Island. Ringing projects in recent years have shown Cabrera to be a magnet for migrants, most of which concentrate in this valley. The archipelago also has major colonies of Mediterranean and Cory's Shearwater, and over 40 pairs of Eleonora's Falcon.*

Map 14. The principal valley of Cabrera Island; inset, the Cabrera Archipelago National Park.

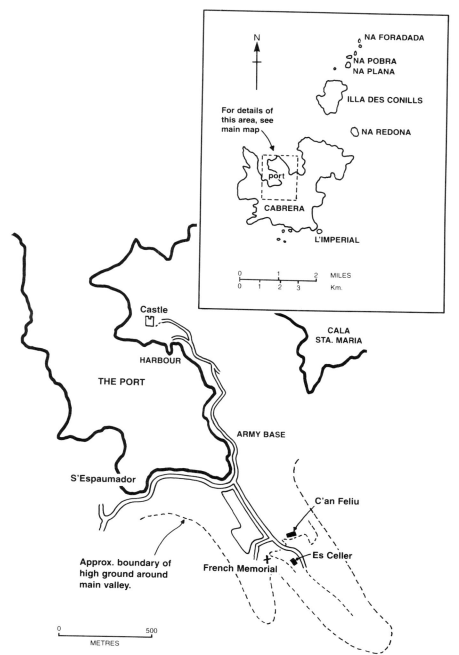

Note that on the way to Colonia Sant Jordi for the Cabrera boat, you pass very close to the salinas in Colonia itself, and the Salinas de Levante a little further north. A brief visit to one or both of these sites could be combined with a Cabrera trip if time permits.

Other sites

Cabo Blanco

This headland, situated in the south-west of the island, is poorly known ornithologically, due at least in part to its relative inaccessability from Puerto Pollensa/Alcudia, where most birders base themselves. Nevertheless, Cabo Blanco (or Cap Blanc) has turned up several interesting records despite minimal coverage, and appears to have considerable potential. Furthermore, the site is good for Thekla Lark and is one of the best areas on Mallorca for Marmora's Warbler. The cliffs below the headland hold the most important breeding colony of Shag in the Balearics (about 200 breeding pairs). As with many Mallorcan headlands, it is rather too high above sea level for good seawatching, but it is certainly no worse than, for example, Cabo Formentor or Capdepera. Its situation on the south-west coast suggests it ought to be good for migrants, especially in spring, and records of Mallorcan sub-rarities such as Merlin and Whimbrel from Cabo Blanco tend to confirm this.

Access to the area around the lighthouse is off the coast road on the very sharp bend at about K18.1. This area holds Thekla Lark, some Marmora's Warblers, and is the best for migrants. Some caution is required as the area immediately north of the lighthouse is a military zone, so pay heed to any "Zona Militar" signs and fences around here. To the north where the coast road runs close to the cliff edge it is again possible to pull over (at K16.5), and there is an excellent scrub area here which holds Marmora's Warbler.

Dragonera

Dragonera is a small island close to the extreme western tip of Mallorca. Its principal importance lies with its breeding birds: the sheer cliffs on the north side hold about fifty pairs of Eleonora's Falcon (the most important colony in Mallorca), Marmora's Warbler is common throughout, and there is an Audouin's Gull colony of about 100 pairs. In addition, recent ringing campaigns held by GOB on the island in autumn have demonstrated its potential as a migration trap, with such major national rarities as Common Rosefinch and Red-breasted Flycatcher having been caught here. Certainly if based in the extreme west of Mallorca, it would be well-worth considering a trip to Dragonera.

Access to the island is provided by boats which depart trom Sant Elm and also from Puerto Andratx. Boats to the island usually only run in the summer months (May-September) at the time of writing, but there are several crossings every day, and it may be possible to arrange crossings for other times of the year, certainly for a group. We strongly advise that you check locally (and/or at your hotel) for details of getting to Dragonera, as access to the island is subject to change without notice. There is no food or drink available on the island, so visitors must take these with them.

Birdwise, the boat crossing is often very good for views of shearwaters and other sea-birds. On the island, around the harbour, both Marmora's Warbler and Blue Rock Thrush can be easily seen. Following the main track that leads to the southern lighthouse brings you to some terraced fields and groves after a few hundred metres, and this is the best area to look for migrants in the appropriate seasons. Eleonora's Falcons are likey to be seen anywhere on the island between May and early November, but the best viewing area for the breeding cliffs is another 2 km south shortly before the lighthouse, where the track comes close the cliff edge. Allowing time for birding, at least two hours should be allowed for this walk, as the track is quite winding in places. The shorter walk to the northern lighthouse takes you past the Audouin's Gull breeding colony (on the lower ridge to the south of the track), but there are usually some present in this area year-round.

Embalse de Casablanca

This is a relatively new reservoir constructed to the north of the airport. So far it has received virtually no coverage by birders, but despite its small size can hold reasonable numbers of wildfowl. Above all, it has potential as there are so few water bodies in the west of the island, and its proximity to the airport and Palma make it easy to check when passing to and from that part of the island. There is so little information for this site it is impossible to give anything more than a hint as to what could be seen there. Any of the island's wildfowl species are possible, with Shoveler, Tufted Duck, Wigeon and Pochard wintering there in small numbers, and Yellow-legged and Black-headed Gulls visit in good numbers, so any other gull species is also possible. Black-necked Grebe has been seen there in winter. The banks are artificial and rather steep, so it is unlikely to hold waders for any length of time, but waders will nevertheless drop in briefly on passage, and the banks may be particularly attractive to pratincoles.

Access is off the C-715 Palma-Manacor road. Heading from the Palma ring road towards Manacor on the C-715, carry on through Son Ferriol and take the left-hand turn at K7.0. Staying on this road, you arrive at the reservoir (on your right) after about 1.5 km. If you should miss this turn, then an alternative is to carry on to the village Sa Casa Blanca and turn left just as you are about to leave the village, at the Bar Can Rigan. This turning is opposite a right-hand turn marked to Sant Jordi, which is one of several roads that can be easily used for getting to the airport. If taking the Sa Casa Blanca turning to the reservoir, again follow the road north round to a tiny village with paved roads, at which point bear left, and after about 0.5 km the reservoir appears on your left.

View the reservoir from the roads which run around three sides of the site, the north side affording the best views. This is a private site which is well-fenced, and the as whole site can be seen very well from the road, entry is both illegal and wholly unnecessary.

Other fauna and flora in Mallorca

In addition to its birds, Mallorca is also very popular for its wild flowers. This is due to the considerable number of endemic species found here, typical of a remote Mediterranean island, as well as a good selection of Mediterranean orchids. The best time to come looking for flowers is from late March to late April, whilst the best area in which to base oneself is again the north-east of the island. Although the location of the base area is not so vital as for the birds, being close to the mountains is desirable as this is where the rare endemic species are mostly to be found. This is not the book to list the flowers in detail, but we can thoroughly recommend the "Illustrated Flora of Mallorca" by Dr. Elspeth Beckett. "Mediterranean Wild Flowers" (Blamey and Grey-Wilson 1993) is an excellent general guide the flowers of the region.

Mammals are generally scarce in Mallorca as all the large mammals were hunted to extinction early after man's colonisation of the island. Today only a handful of smaller species remain; the North African sub-species of Hedgehog is found island-wide, but is invariably only encountered dead on the roadside. The Pine Marten is rarely seen but is reasonably common in the mountains and foothills. Genet is also present, but being nocturnal is even more rarely seen than the Pine Marten. The only other predators are Wild Cat (but its status is poorly known), and the Weasel, which is found throughout the island. Other mammals include Rabbit, Hare, Garden Dormouse, Rat, Water Vole, Field Mouse, and bats. The latter are well-represented on the island (about 9 species), but are poorly known.

Snakes are represented by only four species, and all are non-poisonous. The most common is the Viperine Snake found mostly in the Albufera marshes, although it can also be found in mountain andwooded regions. The others are: Grass Snake, found only in S'Albufera and occasionally growing to a length of two metres, Cowl Snake and Ladder-back Snake, the latter two being very rare.

Amphibians are represented by Marsh Frogs, and an endemic species of Midwife Toad, found only in a few sites in the mountains. Geckos, both Moorish and Disc-fingered, are quite common, the latter being partial to human habitation and very useful in keeping down flies and mosquitoes. Lilford's Lizard is another Balearic endemic found on Cabrera with another sub-species being found on Dragonera.

Butterflies and moths are reasonably well represented on this offshore island with Swallowtail, Cleopatra, Two-tailed Pasha, Clouded Yellow and a variety of blue butterflies usually in evidence in season, as well as some of the hawk moths including Deaths Head. There is also a good selection of dragonflies, damselflies, hymenoptera, beetles etc., certainly enough for the most dedicated naturalist.

References

Beckett, E. 1993. Illustrated Flora of Mallorca. Editorial Moll, Palma.

Blamey, M. & Grey-Wilson, C. 1993. Mediterranean Wild Flowers. Harper-Collins London.

Parker, J. 1991. Walking in Mallorca. Cicerone Press, Cumbria.

King, J. R. & Hearl, G. in prep. Birds of the Balearic Islands. T. & A. D. Poyser, London.

Checklist of the Birds of Mallorca

This list includes all 314 species that have been recorded in Mallorca for which there is adequate documentation. The order follows that of Voous, and the chosen English names are those preferred by the authors.

The status codes used are defined below. It is clear however that these are greatly simplified, and it is possible to find straggling individuals of a wintering species in mid–summer, or vice versa. Equally, the status of a species may change. While this often as a result of improved knowledge, there is also a continuous pattern of colonisation and extinction of breeding species, as is typical for many islands. Some of this colonisation has occurred naturally (e.g. by Starling in recent years), but some other species have been (re)introduced by man, as part of deliberate programmes, and these are also indicated.

For species marked as vagrants (V), all records should be accompanied by a full description for consideration by the CHRM (regional records committee), whilst those marked V* are national rarities, records of which are considered by the CIR, the Iberian Rarities Committee. Records of rare migrants (RM) are likely to require some supporting notes for the CHRM. Details submitted to Graham Hearl will be forwarded to the relevant authorities (see Introduction).

R	Resident	RM	Rare Migrant
S	Summer	V	Vagrant
W	Winter	?	status requiring clarification
M	Migrant	( )	presumed escapes from captivity
Ms	Migrant, mainly in spring	I	Introduced or reintroduced
Ma	Migrant, mainly in autumn		

BEA.

English name	Scientific name	Status
Red-throated Diver	*Gavia stellata*	V
Black-throated Diver	*Gavia arctica*	V
Great Northern Diver	*Gavia immer*	V
Little Grebe	*Tachybaptus ruficollis*	R
Great Crested Grebe	*Podiceps cristatus*	W
Red-necked Grebe	*Podiceps grisegena*	V
Slavonian Grebe	*Podiceps auritus*	V*
Black-necked Grebe	*Podiceps nigricollis*	W, Ma
Cory's Shearwater	*Calonectris diomedea*	R
Mediterranean Shearwater	*Puffinus yelkouan*	R
Storm Petrel	*Hydrobates pelagicus*	S
Gannet	*Morus bassanus*	RM
Cormorant	*Phalacrocorax carbo*	W
Shag	*Phalacrocorax aristotelis*	R
White Pelican	*Pelecanus onocrotalus*	V*
Bittern	*Botaurus stellaris*	S
Little Bittern	*Ixobrychus minutus*	S
Night Heron	*Nycticorax nycticorax*	R
Squacco Heron	*Ardeola ralloides*	Ms
Cattle Egret	*Bubulcus ibis*	R
Little Egret	*Egretta garzetta*	R
Great White Egret	*Egretta alba*	RM
Grey Heron	*Ardea cinerea*	R
Purple Heron	*Ardea purpurea*	S
Black Stork	*Ciconia nigra*	RM
White Stork	*Ciconia ciconia*	RM
Glossy Ibis	*Plegadis falcinellus*	RM
Sacred Ibis	*Threskiornis aethiopicus*	(V)*
Spoonbill	*Platalea leucorodia*	RM
African Spoonbill	*Platalea alba*	(V)*
Greater Flamingo	*Phoenicopterus ruber*	RM
Lesser Flamingo	*Phoenicopterus minor*	(V)*
Mute Swan	*Cygnus olor*	(V)
White-fronted Goose	*Anser albifrons*	V
Greylag Goose	*Anser anser*	W
Ruddy Shelduck	*Tadorna ferruginea*	V*
Shelduck	*Tadorna tadorna*	RM
Mandarin Duck	*Aix galericulata*	(V)
Wigeon	*Anas penelope*	W
Gadwall	*Anas strepera*	W
Teal	*Anas crecca*	W
Mallard	*Anas platyrhynchos*	R
Pintail	*Anas acuta*	W
Garganey	*Anas querquedula*	Ms
Shoveler	*Anas clypeata*	W
Marbled Teal	*Marmaronetta angustirostris*	V
Red-crested Pochard	*Netta rufina*	I
Pochard	*Aythya ferina*	W, R?
Ferruginous Duck	*Aythya nyroca*	RM, I
Tufted Duck	*Aythya fuligula*	W

English name	Scientific name	Status
Scaup	*Aythya marila*	V
Long-tailed Duck	*Clangula hyemalis*	V
Common Scoter	*Melanitta nigra*	V
Red-breasted Merganser	*Mergus serrator*	V
Goosander	*Mergus merganser*	V*
White-headed Duck	*Oxyura leucocephala*	I
Honey Buzzard	*Pernis apivorus*	Ms
Black Kite	*Milvus migrans*	M
Red Kite	*Milvus milvus*	R
Egyptian Vulture	*Neophron percnopterus*	R
Griffon Vulture	*Gyps fulvus*	R
Black Vulture	*Aegypius monachus*	R
Short-toed Eagle	*Circaetus gallicus*	V
Marsh Harrier	*Circus aeruginosus*	R
Hen Harrier	*Circus cyaneus*	W
Pallid Harrier	*Circus macrourus*	V*
Montagu's Harrier	*Circus pygargus*	Ms
Sparrowhawk	*Accipiter nisus*	RM
Common Buzzard	*Buteo buteo*	M, W
Golden Eagle	*Aquila chrysaetos*	V
Lesser Spotted Eagle	*Aquila pomarina*	V*
Booted Eagle	*Heiraaetus pennatus*	R
Bonelli's Eagle	*Heiraaetus fasciatus*	V
Osprey	*Pandion haliaetus*	R
Lesser Kestrel	*Falco naumanni*	V
Kestrel	*Falco tinnunculus*	R
Red-footed Falcon	*Falco vespertinus*	Ms
Merlin	*Falco columbarius*	RM
Hobby	*Falco subbuteo*	RM
Eleonora's Falcon	*Falco eleonorae*	S
Lanner	*Falco biarmicus*	V*
Saker	*Falco cherrug*	V*
Peregrine	*Falco peregrinus*	R
Barbary Falcon	*Falco pelegrinoides*	V*
Red-legged Partridge	*Alectoris rufa*	R
Quail	*Coturnix coturnix*	S
Pheasant	*Phasianus colchicus*	R
Water Rail	*Rallus aquaticus*	R
Spotted Crake	*Porzana porzana*	M
Little Crake	*Porzana parva*	V
Baillon's Crake	*Porzana pusilla*	V
Corncrake	*Crex crex*	V
Moorhen	*Gallinula chloropus*	R
Purple Gallinule	*Porphyrio porphyrio*	I
Coot	*Fulica atra*	R
Common Crane	*Grus grus*	RM
Oystercatcher	*Haematopus ostralegus*	RM
Black-winged Stilt	*Himantopus himantopus*	R
Avocet	*Recurvirostra avosetta*	M
Stone Curlew	*Burhinus oedicnemus*	R

English name	Scientific name	Status
Collared Pratincole	*Glareola pratincola*	Ms
Black-winged Pratincole	*Glareola nordmanni*	V*
Little Ringed Plover	*Charadrius dubius*	S, R?
Ringed Plover	*Charadrius hiaticula*	M
Kentish Plover	*Charadrius alexandrinus*	R
Dotterel	*Charadrius morinellus*	V
Golden Plover	*Pluvialis apricaria*	W
Grey Plover	*Pluvialis squatarola*	W
Lapwing	*Vanellus vanellus*	W
Knot	*Calidris canutus*	RM
Sanderling	*Calidris alba*	RM
Little Stint	*Calidris minuta*	M, W
Temminck's Stint	*Calidris temminckii*	RM
White-rumped Sandpiper	*Calidris fuscicollis*	V*
Pectoral Sandpiper	*Calidris melanotos*	V*
Curlew Sandpiper	*Calidris ferruginea*	M
Purple Sandpiper	*Calidris maritima*	V
Dunlin	*Calidris alpina*	M, W
Broad-billed Sandpiper	*Limicola falcinellus*	V*
Stilt Sandpiper	*Micropalama himantopus*	V*
Ruff	*Philomachus pugnax*	M, W
Jack Snipe	*Lymnocriptes minimus*	W
Snipe	*Gallinago gallinago*	W
Great Snipe	*Gallinago media*	V*
Woodcock	*Scolopax rusticola*	W
Black-tailed Godwit	*Limosa limosa*	M
Bar-tailed Godwit	*Limosa lapponica*	RM
Whimbrel	*Numenius phaeopus*	Ma
Curlew	*Numenius arquata*	W
Spotted Redshank	*Tringa erythropus*	M, W
Redshank	*Tringa totanus*	M, W
Marsh Sandpiper	*Tringa stagnatilis*	M
Greenshank	*Tringa nebularia*	M
Lesser Yellowlegs	*Tringa flavipes*	V*
Green Sandpiper	*Tringa ochropus*	M, W
Wood Sandpiper	*Tringa glareola*	M
Terek Sandpiper	*Xenus cinereus*	V*
Common Sandpiper	*Actitis hypoleucos*	M, W
Turnstone	*Arenaria interpres*	RM
Red-necked Phalarope	*Phalaropus lobatus*	V
Arctic Skua	*Stercorarius parasiticus*	V
Long-tailed Skua	*Stercorarius longicaudus*	V*
Great Skua	*Stercorarius skua*	V
Mediterranean Gull	*Larus melanocephalus*	RM
Little Gull	*Larus minutus*	RM
Black-headed Gull	*Larus ridibundus*	W, M
Slender-billed Gull	*Larus genei*	RM
Audouin's Gull	*Larus audouinii*	R
Common Gull	*Larus canus*	V
Lesser Black-backed Gull	*Larus fuscus*	RM

English name	Scientific name	Status
Yellow-legged Gull	*Larus cachinnans*	R
Iceland Gull	*Larus glaucoides*	V*
Glaucous Gull	*Larus hyperboreus*	V*
Great Black-backed Gull	*Larus marinus*	V
Kittiwake	*Rissa tridactyla*	V
Gull-billed Tern	*Gelochelidon nilotica*	Ms
Caspian Tern	*Sterna caspia*	V*
Sandwich Tern	*Sterna sandvicensis*	W
Roseate Tern	*Sterna dougallii*	V
Common Tern	*Sterna hirundo*	RM
Little Tern	*Sterna albifrons*	Ms
Whiskered Tern	*Chlidonias hybridus*	Ms
Black Tern	*Chlidonias niger*	Ms
White-winged Black Tern	*Chlidonias leucopterus*	Ms
Guillemot	*Uria aalge*	V
Razorbill	*Alca torda*	V
Puffin	*Fratercula arctica*	W
Rock-Dove	*Columba livia*	R
Stock Dove	*Columba oenas*	V
Woodpigeon	*Columba palumbus*	R
African Collared Dove	*Streptopelia roseogrisea*	I
Turtle Dove	*Streptopelia turtur*	S
Great Spotted Cuckoo	*Clamator glandarius*	V
Cuckoo	*Cuculus canorus*	S
Barn Owl	*Tyto alba*	R
Scops Owl	*Otus scops*	R
Little Owl	*Athene noctua*	R?
Long-eared Owl	*Asio otus*	R
Short-eared Owl	*Asio flammeus*	RM
Nightjar	*Caprimulgus europaeus*	M, S?
Red-necked Nightjar	*Caprimulgus ruficollis*	V
Swift	*Apus apus*	S
Pallid Swift	*Apus pallidus*	S
Alpine Swift	*Apus melba*	M, S
Kingfisher	*Alcedo atthis*	W
Bee-eater	*Merops apiaster*	S
Roller	*Coracias garrulus*	RM
Hoopoe	*Upupa epops*	R
Wryneck	*Jynx torquilla*	R
Bar-tailed Desert Lark	*Ammomanes cincturus*	V*
Short-toed Lark	*Calandrella brachydactyla*	S
Lesser Short-toed Lark	*Calandrella rufescens*	V
Thekla Lark	*Galerida theklae*	R
Woodlark	*Lullula arborea*	V
Skylark	*Alauda arvensis*	W
Sand Martin	*Riparia riparia*	M
Crag Martin	*Ptyonoprogne rupestris*	R
Swallow	*Hirundo rustica*	S
Red-rumped Swallow	*Hirundo daurica*	Ms
House Martin	*Delichon urbica*	S

English name	Scientific name	Status
Richard's Pipit	*Anthus novaeseelandiae*	V*
Tawny Pipit	*Anthus campestris*	S
Olive-backed Pipit	*Anthus hodgsoni*	V*
Tree Pipit	*Anthus trivialis*	M
Meadow Pipit	*Anthus pratensis*	W
Red-throated Pipit	*Anthus cervinus*	Ms
Water Pipit	*Anthus spinoletta*	W
Yellow Wagtail	*Motacilla flava*	S, M
Citrine Wagtail	*Motacilla citreola*	V*
Grey Wagtail	*Motacilla cinerea*	W
White Wagtail	*Motacilla alba*	W
Wren	*Troglodytes troglodytes*	R
Dunnock	*Prunella modularis*	W
Alpine Accentor	*Prunella collaris*	W
Rufous Bush Chat	*Cercotrichas galactotes*	V
Robin	*Erithacus rubecula*	W
Nightingale	*Luscinia megarhynchos*	S
Bluethroat	*Luscinia svecica*	W
Black Redstart	*Phoenicurus ochruros*	W
Redstart	*Phoenicurus phoenicurus*	M
Whinchat	*Saxicola rubetra*	M
Stonechat	*Saxicola torquata*	R
Northern Wheatear	*Oenanthe oenanthe*	M
Black-eared Wheatear	*Oenanthe hispanica*	Ms
Rock Thrush	*Monticola saxatilis*	S
Blue Rock Thrush	*Monticola solitarius*	R
White's Thrush	*Zoothera dauma*	V*
Ring Ouzel	*Turdus torquatus*	W
Blackbird	*Turdus merula*	R
Fieldfare	*Turdus pilaris*	W
Song Thrush	*Turdus philomelos*	W
Redwing	*Turdus iliacus*	W
Mistle Thrush	*Turdus viscivorus*	W
Cetti's Warbler	*Cettia cetti*	R
Fan-tailed Warbler	*Cisticola juncidis*	R
Grasshopper Warbler	*Locustella naevia*	RM
Savi's Warbler	*Locustella luscinioides*	V
Moustached Warbler	*Acrocephalus melanopogon*	R
Aquatic Warbler	*Acrocephalus paludicola*	V
Sedge Warbler	*Acrocephalus schoenobaenus*	RM
Marsh Warbler	*Acrocephalus palustris*	V*
Reed Warbler	*Acrocephalus scirpaceus*	S
Great Reed Warbler	*Acrocephalus arundinaceus*	S
Olivaceous Warbler	*Hippolais pallida*	RM
Icterine Warbler	*Hippolais icterina*	Ms
Melodious Warbler	*Hippolais polyglotta*	Ms
Marmora's Warbler	*Sylvia sarda*	R
Dartford Warbler	*Sylvia undata*	W
Spectacled Warbler	*Sylvia conspicillata*	S
Subalpine Warbler	*Sylvia cantillans*	M, S

English name	Scientific name	Status
Sardinian Warbler	*Sylvia melanocephala*	R
Orphean Warbler	*Sylvia hortensis*	V
Barred Warbler	*Sylvia nisoria*	V*
Lesser Whitethroat	*Sylvia curruca*	V
Whitethroat	*Sylvia communis*	M
Garden Warbler	*Sylvia borin*	M
Blackcap	*Sylvia atricapilla*	R
Yellow-browed Warbler	*Phylloscopus inornatus*	V*
Bonelli's Warbler	*Phylloscopus bonelli*	Ms
Wood Warbler	*Phylloscopus sibilatrix*	M
Chiffchaff	*Phylloscopus collybita*	W
Willow Warbler	*Phylloscopus trochilus*	M
Goldcrest	*Regulus regulus*	W
Firecrest	*Regulus ignicapillus*	R
Spotted Flycatcher	*Muscicapa striata*	S
Red-breasted Flycatcher	*Ficedula parva*	V*
Collared Flycatcher	*Ficedula albicollis*	V*
Pied Flycatcher	*Ficedula hypoleuca*	M, S
Blue Tit	*Parus caeruleus*	R
Coal Tit	*Parus ater*	V
Great Tit	*Parus major*	R
Wallcreeper	*Tichodroma muraria*	V
Short-toed Treecreeper	*Certhia brachydactyla*	V
Penduline Tit	*Remiz pendulinus*	W
Golden Oriole	*Oriolus oriolus*	Ms
Red-backed Shrike	*Lanius collurio*	RM
Great Grey Shrike	*Lanius excubitor*	V
Masked Shrike	*Lanius nubicus*	V*
Woodchat Shrike	*Lanius senator*	S
Magpie	*Pica pica*	(V)
Alpine Chough	*Pyrrhocorax graculus*	V
Chough	*Pyrrhocorax pyrrhocorax*	V
Jackdaw	*Corvus monedula*	V
Rook	*Corvus frugilegus*	V
Carrion Crow	*Corvus corone*	V
Raven	*Corvus corax*	R
Starling	*Sturnus vulgaris*	R
Spotless Starling	*Sturnus unicolor*	RM?
Rose-coloured Starling	*Sturnus roseus*	V*
House Sparrow	*Passer domesticus*	R
Spanish Sparrow	*Passer hispaniolensis*	V?
Tree Sparrow	*Passer montanus*	RM?
Rock Sparrow	*Petronia petronia*	RM?.
Snow Finch	*Montifringilla nivalis*	V
Chaffinch	*Fringilla coelebs*	R
Brambling	*Fringilla montifringilla*	RM
Serin	*Serinus serinus*	R
Greenfinch	*Carduelis chloris*	R
Goldfinch	*Carduelis carduelis*	R
Siskin	*Carduelis spinus*	W

English name	Scientific name	Status
Linnet	*Carduelis cannabina*	R
Crossbill	*Loxia curvirostra*	R
Trumpeter Finch	*Bucanetes githagineus*	V
Common Rosefinch	*Cardopacus erythrinus*	V*
Hawfinch	*Coccothraustes coccothraustes*	W
Snow Bunting	*Plectrophenax nivalis*	V
Yellowhammer	*Emberiza citrinella*	V
Cirl Bunting	*Emberiza cirlus*	R
Rock Bunting	*Emberiza cia*	V
Ortolan Bunting	*Emberiza hortulana*	M
Little Bunting	*Emberiza pusilla*	V*
Reed Bunting	*Emberiza schoeniclus*	R
Black-headed Bunting	*Emberiza melanocephala*	V*
Corn Bunting	*Miliaria calandra*	R

NOTES

NOTES

NOTES

NOTES